BUSINESS CYCLES AND EQUILIBRIUM

Business Cycles and Equilibrium

FISCHER BLACK

Basil Blackwell

Basil Blackwell Inc.
432 Park Avenue South, Suite 1503
New York, NY 10016, USA

Basil Blackwell Ltd
108 Cowley Road, Oxford, OX4 1JF, UK

Library of Congress Cataloging-in-Publication Data

Black, Fischer
 Business cycles and equilibrium
 Includes index
 1. Business cycles 2. Equilibrium (Economics)
 I. Title
 HB3711.B497 1987   338.5′42   87-6578
 ISBN 0-631-15754-9 (US)

British Library Cataloguing in Publication Data

Black, Fischer
 Business cycles and equilibrium.
 1. Equilibrium (Economics)
 I. Title
 330.15′43   HB145
 ISBN 0-631-15754-9

Phototypeset by Dobbie Typesetting Service,
Plymouth, Devon, England
Printed in the USA

Contents

Introduction

Since the late 1960s I have been working on theories that depend on the idea that economic and financial markets are in continual equilibrium. Equilibrium means there are no opportunities to make abnormal profits; more generally, it means that there are no easy ways for people to shift positions in a way that makes everyone better off.

Equilibrium was the concept that attracted me to finance and economics. I have never had a course in either subject. While working at Arthur D. Little in 1966, I met Jack Treynor, who began telling me about an equilibrium theory he was working on called the capital asset pricing model. I was hooked.

I began doing research in finance, and later in economics. I started doing consulting in finance. I was especially interested in applying the idea of continual equilibrium to all kinds of markets. I found it stimulating to combine consulting and research: most of the key concepts in my work were developed at this time, before I went to the University of Chicago to start my academic career.

The capital asset pricing model was first applied to stocks, but I wanted to apply it to other securities, like options and bonds. In trying to apply it to options, Myron Scholes and I found an option pricing formula. In trying to apply it to bonds, I developed the notion that monetary policy is and must be passive in an economy with well-developed financial markets.

This research on monetary policy and banking led to my first published paper, which begins this volume. I continued looking for a model that would allow markets to be in continual equilibrium while leaving a way for the government to control the money stock, but I was never able to find one. I decided that monetary policy can influence neither output nor prices.

At first I felt that the government could not influence interest rates through open market operations, but I changed that view over time.

I became convinced that it takes time for people to respond to certain events even when markets are in continual equilibrium. This allows the government to force the federal funds rate above or below its natural level while the government is intervening actively in debt markets, but only if it forces other interest rates in the opposite direction. I still believe that the government has no control over "the" interest rate through monetary policy.

This work on monetary theory led me into research on business cycles. If monetary policy does not influence the economy, what does? I decided that business cycles are a natural result of uncertainty in a general equilibrium model. I see no need to assume sticky prices or easily corrected ignorance or government-influenced aggregate demand to explain business cycles.

At first I put some emphasis on rational expectations in my theories. Later I decided I didn't need that assumption. My key assumption now is simply that markets are in continual equilibrium. Some people may be confused, and others may have odd-looking objectives, but so long as prices and quantities are free to move, we are in a general equilibrium world.

While I don't believe the government can do much with open market operations, I do think it has some influence on the economy through taxes and regulations. Changes in taxes and regulations may even play a small role in business cycles. Taxes can also be used to affect the balance of trade with other countries, though I don't think the balance of trade affects our welfare in any particular way.

Though I think monetary policy is ineffective in a country with well-developed financial markets, I believe that when the government in a country with more primitive markets prints money and spends it, the inflation rate will rise. Hyperinflation will be a common result.

I'm not sure we should say that it's monetary policy that causes the hyperinflation. A government that prints money and spends it is usually creating massive deficits at the same time. Perhaps we should say that fiscal policy causes the hyperinflation. In any case, a government that prints massive amounts of money to spend will usually cause both hyperinflation and a general breakdown in financial markets.

My research on monetary theory and business cycles led to work on the balance of payments and the world business cycle. I was unable to find any interesting definition of the balance of payments other than the net flow of gold out of a country, and even that has no obvious impact on the country's welfare.

The idea that the business cycle is just a way of looking at an economy in general equilibrium leads naturally to the world business cycle as a reflection of world general equilibrium. In countries that produce mostly a few products or services, it is especially clear that changes in overall supply and demand factors can explain business cycles without the need for devices like sticky prices.

The idea that the world general equilibrium is independent of monetary factors is a sophisticated version of purchasing power parity. It says that the paths of real output and relative prices will be unaffected by the paths of the price level and exchange rates. Government intervention in the foreign exchange market can affect exchange rates and therefore inflation rates, but this will not cause the path of total real output or the composition of real output or relative prices to be different than they would otherwise have been.

With fixed exchange rates, inflation rates in different countries will be tied together. They will not be the same, but if inflation in one country is higher than it would otherwise have been, inflation in other countries will be higher than it would otherwise have been. With flexible exchange rates, exchange rate variations can cause price level variations in the same sense, but it seems more likely that price level variations will cause exchange rate variations. That is, when the price level in one country is higher than it would otherwise have been, the exchange rates for that country with other countries will be lower than they would otherwise have been.

Nominal interest rates and inflation rates will be connected in a similar way. When the nominal interest rate is higher than it would otherwise have been, the inflation rate using any price index will be higher than it would otherwise have been, though the higher nominal interest rate is not likely to be a direct cause of the higher inflation rate. I believe that monetary policy is passive, and therefore affects neither real nor nominal quantities. In particular, it has no effect on interest rates, exchange rates, or the inflation rate.

But if monetary policy doesn't affect the inflation rate, what does?

At first I said that changes in the inflation rate are caused by non-monetary factors such as changes in relative prices. I outlined a theory of inflation in which an increase or decrease in the price of oil will cause an increase or decrease in the inflation rate, other things equal. Later I added expectations as an important causal factor. In the theories in this book, the price level and inflation rate and exchange rates are indeterminate. In the world, though, they are determined, and I now think that expectations play an important role.

In a real sense, inflation can be whatever we expect it will be, even when our expectations are based on the incorrect view that the government can control inflation through open market operations.

There was a time, though, when we had a gold standard, which seems to rule out a role for expectations. If relative prices are given by the real equilibrium, then fixing the dollar price of a single good will fix the dollar prices of all goods. None of the prices will be constant, but they will all be determined by the price of gold.

Thus I decided that the government can control the price level by standing ready to buy or sell gold at a fixed price. Since the government can use this process to fix the price of gold at a point in time, it can adjust the fixed price of gold over time to stabilize a general price index.

Only standing ready to buy or sell gold will do it: the government cannot just pass a law specifying the price of gold, since that would soon cause almost all transactions in gold to stop. And since monetary policy must still be passive in my world, controlling the price of gold acts directly on the price level, rather than acting through monetary policy.

In a "small country," controlling the exchange rate can be as effective as controlling the price of gold. Even a large country can influence its inflation rate to some degree if it intervenes in foreign exchange markets.

In foreign exchange markets, the government can control exchange rates without holding much currency, since currency can always be exchanged for other assets. Similarly, the government can apparently control the price of gold without holding much gold, and without fear of running out of gold, since it can always exchange gold and other assets.

This leads to the puzzling notion that the government stands ready to buy or sell gold at a price that is fixed at each moment, while at the same time adjusting any surplus or deficiency in its stock of gold by exchanging it for other assets. Or the same thing with foreign exchange if it is fixing exchange rates. If this is possible, then the government can control the path of the price level indefinitely.

Buying and selling gold or foreign exchange can be costly, though. The government bears direct and indirect transaction costs, especially when there is "pressure" on the price level or exchange rate. Since the gains from stabilizing the price level or inflation rate are hard to pin down, the government may decide to let the inflation rate and exchange rates wander about rather than trying to control them.

More recently, I have come to believe that speculative prices contain "noise" introduced by those who trade on mistaken beliefs. In a somewhat similar way, prices of goods and services contain noise introduced by the investment decisions of those who do not act rationally. I think this will change the character of business cycles to some degree, perhaps making the fluctuations larger than they might otherwise be. But I don't think it creates an opportunity for the government to improve welfare in some sense.

Even in the presence of noise, I believe that the business cycle is a way of looking at the evolution of a world in general equilibrium; that monetary policy normally influences neither the business cycle nor the inflation rate; and that a gold standard with a changing price of gold, but a stable inventory of gold, could be used to control the inflation rate, but won't be.

The idea that the business cycle is just an aspect of general equilibrium contrasts with most economists' views of business cycles. Can't we do some econometric tests to tell whose ideas are right? Perhaps, but I haven't been able to think of any. Econometric tests can tell us a lot about correlations, but we want to know about causation. We want to know what causes the business cycle, what causes fluctuations in the trade balance, and what influences inflation and interest rates.

I have used mostly verbal rather than mathematical descriptions of my views of business cycles. If we were going to apply statistical tests to these theories, we would try to create a mathematical description of some kind. Since I haven't been able to think of any relevant statistical tests, I'm not sure what good that would do. More important, I think creating a mathematical description would tempt us to become too specific. We would claim that some things are constant, when hardly anything is constant. So I have intentionally left the descriptions mostly verbal.

If my views are correct, there is very little the government should do to influence the economy. Monetary and exchange rate policies accomplish almost nothing, and fiscal policies are unimportant in causing or changing business cycles.

Fischer Black

1

Banking and Interest Rates in a World Without Money: The Effects of Uncontrolled Banking

It is possible to imagine a world in which commercial banks and other financial institutions are free to offer checking accounts (and savings accounts) on any terms they might want to set, and in which there are no reserve requirements. Banks could pay interest on demand deposits, and might not choose to distinguish between demand deposits and time deposits. Since there would be no reserve requirements, there would be no reason for Federal Reserve open market operations.

In such a world, it would not be possible to give any reasonable definition of the quantity of money. The payments mechanism in such a world would be very efficient, but money in the usual sense would not exist. Thus neither the quantity theory of money nor the liquidity preference theory of money would be applicable.

Vickrey was one of the first writers to imagine such a world. He says (1955, p 113):

> In passing it may be noted that the essentially institutional nature of monetary theory, including much of the basic notions of the quantity theory and of the liquidity-preference theory, is brought out by considering how far either of these theories would be applicable to a situation in which all transactions are executed by check or some similar instrument, in which banks cover their operating expenses entirely from service charges and

Reprinted with permission of the Bank Administration Institute from the *Journal of Bank Research*, Autumn, 1970.

pay interest on average balances at rates reflecting the return on their investments, and in which overdrafts are honored fairly freely, possibly at graduated interest rates. It seems likely that for application to such circumstances the theories would have to be rather radically modified, if indeed they did not become entirely inapplicable.

Vickrey does not explore the concept any further in this article, but he has a somewhat longer discussion in a later book (1964, pp. 108–10). There he emphasizes the fact that current monetary theory depends heavily on a rather restricted form of financial institution. He says that other institutional arrangements would make current monetary theory almost completely invalid.

Tobin comes close to saying the same thing several times. In "Commercial Banks as Creators of 'Money'," (1967) he emphasizes the similarity between commercial banks and other financial intermediaries, and thus between the liabilities of commercial banks and the liabilities of other financial intermediaries. He says that the differences would tend to vanish in an unregulated, competitive financial world; and that even in today's world, the volume of liabilities of any financial institution is determined more by depositor preferences than by government and central bank actions. However, Tobin and Brainard say (1967) that the presence of uncontrolled banking reduces, but does not eliminate, the effectiveness of monetary control through changes in the volume of government debt.

Tobin (1968) points out some advantages, at least in a long-run sense, of allowing interest on demand deposits, or allowing interest-bearing assets to serve as means of payment. He says (1968, p. 846):

> Freeing means of payment from the legal limitations of zero interest would make it theoretically possible to have an efficient growth equilibrium without deflation – efficient in the sense that the real rate of interest is high enough to avoid overcapitalization and in the sense that real resources are not diverted into economizing means of payment.

Tobin comes closest to seeing the implications of uncontrolled banking in (1969, p. 26):

If the interest rate on money, as well as the rates on all other financial assets, were flexible and endogenous, then they would all simply adjust to the marginal efficiency of capital. There would be no room for discrepancies between market and natural rates of return on capital, between market valuation and reproduction cost. There would be no room for monetary policy to affect aggregate demand. The real economy would call the tune for the financial sector, with no feedback in the other direction. As previously observed, something like this occurs in the long run, where the influence of monetary policy is not on aggregate demand but on the relative supplies of monetary and real assets, to which all rates of return must adjust.

Gurley and Shaw (1960, pp. 253–6) observe that with laissez-faire banking, the price level is not determinate, and suffers from "aimless drift."

Patinkin (1965, p. 303) also says that the price level is indeterminate when banks are not controlled:

> Indeed, what we have here is the indeterminacy of Wicksell's "pure credit" economy in which all transactions are carried out by checks, while banks hold no reserves. The economic interpretation of this indeterminacy is straightforward: In order for the absolute price level to be determined by market-equilibrating forces, changes in it must impinge on *real* behavior in *some* market, i.e., must create excess demands in some market.

Johnson (1969) and Friedman and Schwartz (1969), on the other hand, claim that uncontrolled banking will lead to an uncontrolled increase in prices. Friedman and Schwartz say (1969, p. 5):

> In the hypothetical world in which there are no costs of setting up a bank and running a bank, and in which deposits transferable by check provide precisely the same services as dominant money, there would be no limit to this process short of a price level of infinity in terms of dominant money.

An even more extreme position is taken by Pesek and Saving (1967), and by Pesek (1968). They say that making money a "free good" (by paying full interest on demand deposits) will make it a worthless good, and will cause a return to barter.

I maintain that the views expressed by Vickrey, Tobin, Gurley and Shaw, and Patinkin are the correct ones. In a world without controls on banking, the real sector will be independent of the financial sector, and the price level will be indeterminate. Traditional monetary theories will be inapplicable; in fact, it will not be possible to define the quantity of money in meaningful terms. Finally, I claim that this world would have several advantages, and few obvious disadvantages, over our present economic and monetary system.

A World Without Money

Let us imagine, then, a world in which money does not exist.

The major financial institutions in this world are banks. There are several competing major banks with branches in every state, as well as banks that are more limited geographically. Payments in this world are made by check. Because of economies of scale in check clearing, there may be only one major clearing corporation, which is operated either by the banks as a group or by the government. We might even imagine that checks have been replaced by an electronic payments mechanism; the discussion below would not be affected by this assumption.

Each bank is allowed to accept deposits under any conditions that it chooses to specify, and to pay any rate of interest on these deposits. In particular, the bank can allow transfers of credit by check between two interest-bearing accounts. Demand deposits will pay interest, and depositors are likely to be charged the full cost of transferring credit from one account to another. Almost all deposits will be in the form of demand deposits.

The banks will make loans to individuals, businesses, and governments. They will probably establish a schedule of interest charges for each borrower, and will then allow him to write checks on his account that increase the amount of his loan whenever he needs the money. The interest rate paid by a borrower will depend on such things as the amount he has borrowed, his wealth, his current income and his future income prospects. It will also depend on the extent to which he provides the bank with collateral for his loan. The banks will also probably set a maximum amount that they will lend to any individual, but this maximum is mainly to keep the borrower from running up a very large debt and then declaring bankruptcy. An individual who intends to repay his loans would not approach the maximum except in very unusual circumstances. Repayment will be flexible; so long as the bank is in touch with the borrower and is satisfied of his ability to repay, he will not need to make payments of principal or interest in any particular month or year. Interest will simply be charged against his account periodically and will serve to increase the amount of his loan.

There will be an active market in inter-bank funds. A bank that has more deposits than loans will deposit its excess funds with other banks that have more loans than deposits. There will be no special reason for an individual bank to have non-bank deposits equal to non-bank loans, since it can adjust any imbalance through transactions with other banks.

Banks will compete in setting schedules of interest rates on loans and in setting transactions charges. The interest rate on deposits will be a standard wholesale money rate. Individuals, corporations, governments, and other banks will all receive the same interest rate on deposits.

Banks will make money on the administration of loans and on the handling of transactions. Their profits on loans will come from the difference between the rates they charge and the wholesale interest rate, minus their expenses. Their profits on transactions will come from the difference between their transactions charges and their costs in handling transactions.

A bank will be happy to bid a customer with positive balances away from another bank, even if it simply redeposits the customer's money with the original bank, because it gets that customer's transactions business (and possibly other business as well). A bank will be happy to bid a customer with negative balances away from another bank, even if it gets the deposits it needs to balance the new loan from the original bank, because it gets both the customer's loan business and the customer's transactions business.

An individual, business, or government will simply have an account at a bank; there will be no need to distinguish between accounts with positive balances (deposits) and accounts with negative balances (loans). An individual may write a check that converts his deposit into a loan, or he may receive a salary payment that converts his loan into a deposit. So long as his loan does not come to exceed the maximum permitted by the bank, there is no need to make special note of these transactions. If his average balance in the latest period is positive, his account will be credited with interest; if his average balance is negative, interest will be charged to his account. Thus there will be no reason for an individual to have both a loan and a deposit at the bank. Since he is allowed to write checks on either a positive or a negative account, and since the interest he pays on his negative account will be greater than the interest he receives on his positive account, he will be better off if he combines the two into a single account.

A business or government account will be handled in the same way as an individual account. The bank will establish a schedule of rates and a maximum loan size, and the account will be allowed to fluctuate freely so long as it does not become a loan larger than the maximum. The business or government can write checks against its account regardless of whether the account has a positive or negative balance.

For the federal government, the interest rate charged on loans will probably be independent of the size of the loan, since there is virtually no risk of default. And there will be no need for an individual bank to set a maximum loan size, since it will probably be happy to loan the government as much as it wants to borrow. The federal government will have very large negative balances at the banks, and will use these bank loans as a substitute for issuing bonds and notes. The total borrowing of the federal government will be limited by Congress, just as it is today. It will be determined by the relation between government outlays and income from taxes and other sources. Massive government spending that is not balanced by taxation would cause the financial system to break down, just as it would cause the existing financial system to break down.

Depositors will be protected in several ways. First of all, every bank will be required to have capital equal to a certain fraction of its loans, and any unusual losses on its loans will come out of that capital. Second, the major banks will be so large that their loan portfolios will be protected by vast diversification. A default on a single loan or on a single group of loans will not be dangerous because it will be such a small fraction of the bank's total portfolio. Finally, the government may provide deposit insurance to protect against catastrophic losses that affect a large fraction of the loans in all banks' portfolios.

Since the banks will not be restricted in making loans to businesses, they will be able to supply the bulk of the loans that businesses need, both short-term and long-term. There will be no reason for businesses to borrow directly by issuing debt securities on the open market; the banks can presumably offer loans at the same interest rate that the market would demand, and the cost of obtaining a bank loan is likely to be less than the cost of a public issue of debt securities. Businesses will obtain part of their capital from bank loans, and the rest from securities, especially common stock. There will be no fixed rule about how much of its capital a business obtains from bank loans; some businesses will have large loans, while others will have none at all. At any time a business can issue common stock to retire some of its loans, or expand its loans to retire some of its common stock.

For the moment, let us suppose that all payments in this simpler world are handled by check or credit card, and that currency is not used. In this world, money does not exist.

An individual has no currency. He has a bank account, but there is no distinction between demand deposits and time deposits. His bank account, if it is positive, represents all of his riskless savings. If it is negative, his bank account represents his borrowing. His bank account together with his holdings of securities and marketable real assets represent his total savings.

There is nothing in this simpler world that can meaningfully be called a quantity of money. Some might say that the total value of all positive bank accounts is the quantity of money. But this makes a completely arbitrary distinction between positive and negative bank accounts. And it means that the quantity of money will change every time an individual transfers credit from his negative bank account to another individual's positive bank account. Others might say that the net value of all bank accounts, both positive and negative, is the quantity of money. But the net value of all the accounts in a bank is simply the capital of that bank. It is equal to the assets of the bank (its loans) minus the liabilities of the bank (its deposits). Thus, the net value of all bank accounts is equal to the aggregate value of all bank securities. We would hardly want to call this the quantity of money.

Still others might say that the value of all potential additional loans in all accounts is the quantity of money. They would say the quantity of money in a positive account is the balance in the account plus the maximum amount the bank would allow the customer to borrow, and the quantity of money in a negative account is the difference between the maximum amount that can be borrowed and the actual amount borrowed. But the maximum size of the loan that is set for a bank customer is arbitrary, and is intended to keep him from intentionally spending himself into bankruptcy. It is not intended to limit the amount of debt he incurs that he will be able to repay. Virtually no individuals will borrow to the maximum, because they will want to have income and borrowing power available for future consumption. So the quantity of money defined in this way will generally have no economic meaning.

There are cases in which this definition of the quantity of money will have economic meaning, however. Suppose, for example, that the maximum loan amount for any individual is set equal to the estimated total value of his wealth, including real assets, financial assets, and the present value of his future income. Then this last definition of the quantity of money will simply be equal to the total wealth of the community. Similarly, if the maximum loan amount is set at a standard percentage of the total value of his human and non-human wealth, this last definition of the quantity of money will be equal to a standard percentage of the total wealth of the community. So although the definition has economic meaning, it is not reasonable to call it the quantity of money.

There are no government bonds, because the government simply borrows from the banks in the same way that individuals and businesses borrow. There is no qualitative difference between government loans and other loans, so there is no reason to treat them differently. Thus, there is no way to include government bonds as part of the quantity of money or the quantity of near money.

Since there is no quantity of money to control, there is no need for a Federal Reserve Board to control it. The banks are not restricted in the amount they can loan by reserve requirements, so there is no need to change their reserve positions through open market operations, or to make changes in the rules relating reserves to total bank assets. The banks may be subject to capital requirements, however. They may be required to have capital equal to some minimum percentage of their loans. But this is not a restriction on the total volume of loans that banks can make, because they can always issue new common stock to raise any additional amounts of capital they may need.

Since there is no quantity of money, it is clear that the quantity of money cannot affect the economy of this world in any way. The quantity of money cannot affect national income, employment, or the rate of inflation, because it does not exist.

We can take one step in the direction of a more complex world by introducing currency. The federal government will print the currency, and will issue it to banks as requested. When a bank receives currency from the government it will credit the government's account by the amount of currency received. The bank will then give the currency to individuals as requested. When a bank gives currency to an individual who has an account with the bank, it will simply reduce his balance by the amount given. When a bank gives currency to an individual in exchange for a check on another bank, it will reduce the balance of the other bank (or increase its balance with the other bank). Thus the amount of currency held by individuals and businesses will be determined by how much it is needed for small payments. So long as the interest rate on bank accounts is positive, an individual will want to hold down the amount of currency that he carries, because currency earns no interest. The amount of currency held by individuals and business will be determined by the volume of small payments, and by the cost and inconvenience of making payment by check or credit card.

The amount of currency held by banks will be determined by the patterns of withdrawals and deposits of currency by individuals and businesses during the day, and by the cost of making transactions with the government. The government will issue currency or retire currency at any time. Thus the amount of currency outstanding at any time will be determined by the needs of individuals and businesses. There will be no need for any federal agency to fix the amount of currency outstanding.

Currency alone can hardly pass for the whole of money. The quantity of currency, in this world, will not be controlled by the central bank, and will not influence the economy. So even when currency is added to our model, the quantity of money can have no effect on output, employment, or prices, because the quantity of money does not exist.

Evolution of the Means of Payment

In this section I want to start with a very simple economy and build up to the whole world without money described above. While there is no money in that world, there is a highly developed means of payment. In the paragraphs that follow I will use the word "money" as short for "means of payment," without meaning to imply that a quantity of money exists in any of these worlds.

Private Business and Commodity Money

In the simplest of all possible worlds there are no financial markets at all. Businesses are owned by individuals and may not be bought or sold. Transactions are made through barter, which is very costly, or through the use of some standard commodities that are compact, portable, and don't deteriorate rapidly. A means of payment that requires transfer of physical commodities is costly because the transfer process is cumbersome, and is extra costly because the commodities, that have value in other uses, must be diverted from these uses to be used as means of payment. Transactions are expensive, and real resources must be tied up for use in making payments.

Common Stock and Portfolio Money

As soon as we introduce any financial market at all, we can eliminate the inefficiencies of barter and commodity money. For example, suppose we introduce common stock. We will allow an individual to sell shares in any businesses he owns, and these shares will trade continuously on the stock market. Shares of common stock may now be used as a means of payment. While it may be possible to use the shares of any company that is traded in the stock market as means of payment, it may be practical to use a standard portfolio of stocks as the means of payment.

Goods may be priced in terms of a unit of account that does not fluctuate in value very much, and the means of payment may be priced in terms of the same unit of account. Thus the dollar price of a share of the standard portfolio will fluctuate from day to day, and even from hour to hour, while the dollar price of a commodity may be relatively stable. This means, of course, that the price of a commodity in terms of shares of the standard portfolio will be constantly fluctuating. This is a slight inconvenience, since it means that every business must be aware of the current dollar price of the standard portfolio, to know how many shares to take in payment for any item. Otherwise, this system would have no disadvantage as a means of payment. Currency could be issued representing shares and fractions of a share of the standard portfolio. The only problem would be the necessity of computing a price, in shares of the standard portfolio, at the time of sale. This price would simply be the dollar price of the item divided by the current dollar price of a share in the standard portfolio.

Borrowing, Lending, and Note Money

While shares in a portfolio of common stocks would be quite satisfactory as a means of payment, they would be less satisfactory as the only intangible form of wealth. We would want to introduce borrowing and lending to provide a larger set of alternative forms of wealth, and at the same time we get a new form of means of payment that eliminates the disadvantage of a portfolio of common stocks. A principal reason for introducing borrowing and lending is for the transfer of risk. Some individuals, instead of holding their wealth in common stocks that fluctuate in value, would rather lend part of their wealth to other individuals at a fixed interest rate. Other individuals would want to borrow to increase their holdings of common stocks, if the borrowing rate were reasonable. In effect, the individuals who lend are paying the individuals who borrow to take over some of their risk. The expected return on equity of a lender will be lower than the expected return on equity of a borrower.

Another reason for introducing borrowing and lending is to allow some individuals to spend more than they are earning by borrowing against their future income, and to allow other individuals to spend less than they are earning, and lend the difference.

Business borrowing and lending adds nothing new; it is equivalent to borrowing and lending by the owners of the business. Whatever the reason for the borrowing and lending, we can assume that the borrower writes a personal note and gives it to the lender in exchange for certain assets. The initial lender may be simply the person from whom the borrower wants to buy. The notes that are created by borrowing and lending may now be used as means of payment. They are better as means of payment than shares in a portfolio of common stocks because they do not fluctuate very much in value (assuming that they are short-term notes). On the other hand, notes have the disadvantage that the holder of a personal note can never be sure that it will be redeemed by the writer at maturity. There may be a significant risk of default, and a significant cost of collection of a personal note. (A note would be redeemed at maturity either in notes of other issuers or in common stock of equivalent value.)

Administration of Loans and Guaranteed Money

To get around the problem of default on personal notes, we can introduce "banks" that serve to administer loans and guarantee personal notes. These banks will neither make loans nor accept deposits. They will simply supervise each borrower, and will guarantee that if he doesn't pay off his notes, they will. In return the bank would charge a fee to cover administrative costs and the probability that a borrower will default on his notes. Thus the notes would bear interest at a lower rate than the rate paid by the borrower; the difference would be income to the supervising bank.

Banks would compete by offering low fees to issuers of notes, and by having a reputation for soundness among holders of notes that they have guaranteed. The government might help ensure a bank's solvency by requiring it to have capital equal to a certain percentage of the notes it has guaranteed. Otherwise, there would be no necessity for government regulation of banks.

Payments would be made using guaranteed notes. These notes would be a convenient, low-cost means of payment that would not fluctuate in value appreciably. But they would still have a few disadvantages. The value of a note would change from day to day due to the accrual of interest. The variety of different notes would be a disadvantage, and some notes might be more acceptable than others. The opportunity for theft might be great if individuals carried notes in large denominations from place to place, unless the notes were registered. But registration might be costly.

Checking Accounts and Bank Money

To solve these problems, we allow the banks to participate in the payments mechanism in a unique way. Instead of remaining outstanding, individual notes will be used only temporarily in making payments, and will then be extinguished. Individuals will have bank accounts that will have positive balances for lenders and negative balances for borrowers. Banks will credit interest to accounts with positive balances and will debit interest to accounts with negative balances. The individual will write a note whenever he or she wants to make a payment. This note will be either in the form of a check or in the form of a credit card purchase receipt. The note will serve to credit the balance of the seller and to debit his balance. It will also credit the balance of the seller's bank with his bank. This system will be a convenient, safe, low-cost means of payment.

In none of these five worlds was there any clearly defined quantity of money. The world of private business and commodity money came closest to having a money supply, but even there, a commodity used as means of payment also has other uses, and it may not be clear when it is to be counted as part of the money supply, and when it is to be counted as involved in one of its other uses. Once we introduce financial markets, however, and intangible means of payment, the idea of a "quantity of money" loses its meaning.

In none of these five worlds was there any role for a central bank. And the only effect that the financial sector had on the real sector was that as we go to successively more efficient means of payment, we reduce the cost of making payments and release real resources for other uses. In none of these worlds was there any mechanism that would cause uncontrolled inflation in the absence of a central bank.

Evolution of Central Bank Control

In this section I want to build up the forms of central bank control over the banking system that are used in the United States. It is clear that each of these forms of control has some effect on the banking system; but it is not clear that any of them has any significant effect on the economy as a whole.

Maximum Interest Rates on Deposits

In the world without money described above, deposits earn interest at the wholesale money rate and banks earn a profit on their transactions charges. Competition will force a bank either to pay the wholesale rate on deposits or to compensate for a lower rate by reducing transactions charges. The wholesale rate will be more common, however, because a bank offering a lower rate and lower transactions charges will tend to attract depositors that keep small balances and have many transactions. Such a bank would tend to lose money on its deposit business.

If the central bank is allowed to establish maximum interest rates on deposits, then various distortions will be introduced. A maximum interest rate on deposits is a rather odd notion in this world, because a deposit is simply an account with a positive balance. What sense does it make to have a maximum interest rate on deposits (positive balances) but no maximum interest rate on loans (negative balances)?

If the maximum interest rate is below the natural level of the wholesale money rate, then an imbalance between supply and demand will be created. At that rate, many loans will seem profitable, but few deposits will come in. The economy will tend to revert to the use of individual and business notes for borrowing and lending, rather than the more efficient use of bank accounts. Because of this imbalance between demand for loans and supply of deposits, banks will try to evade the maximum rates by offering services instead of money interest on deposits. They will offer lower transactions charges, financial assistance to businesses, trust department services, and lower rates on loans. This is rather inefficient, of course, and cannot completely eliminate the effects of maximum interest rates, but it seems to eliminate much of the impact of maximum interest rates in the United States, at least in normal times.

What would happen, though, if the maximum rates were effective on most sources of bank deposits? No bank would be able to attract additional funds from these sources by offering higher rates. So the supply of these funds would be strictly limited. To keep loan demand down to a level equal to the supply of funds, the wholesale money rate for banks would increase until the volume of profitable loans was equal to the volume of available deposits. And this is the rate that banks would offer to any sources of funds not subject to the maximum. The spread between the interest rate paid on most deposits and the wholesale money rate would represent an extra source of profit to the banks. So they might not object strenuously to the central bank's setting maximum interest rates on deposits.

It is sometimes claimed that if banks are not allowed to pay interest on deposits, and if there are no reserve requirements, they will create deposits to buy any asset with a positive expected return, thus bidding up the prices of all assets and causing massive inflation. It is claimed that once a bank creates a deposit, it can never be extinguished, so people will use it to try to buy things and will add to the inflationary pressure.

This argument makes no sense at all. First of all, banks cannot generally own real assets (except bank buildings and equipment) or common stocks. So they cannot simply bid up the prices of these assets. What banks can do is offer to make loans at low interest rates. In our world of positive and negative accounts, this would not work, because it would cause the demand for loans to exceed the supply of deposits. Recall that a borrower in this world simply writes a check that adds to his negative balance whenever he needs to make a payment. Making a loan does not involve the simultaneous creation of a negative balance and a positive balance.

Even in a world where checks can be written only on bank accounts with positive balances, banks cannot offer loans at low interest rates. When a bank creates a deposit larger than the individual wants to hold, he can always use it to pay off some of his loan. Or he can lend it to someone else who will pay off his bank loan. Bank deposits can always be extinguished; they can be used to pay off bank loans. If there are more deposits than people want to hold, the banks will discover that their deposits are being used to pay off their loans, and the volume of both will decline. Thus the banking system can be in equilibrium in a world with zero interest on deposits only if the interest rates on bank loans are high.

An individual bank offering lower interest rates on loans than other banks will be able to get loan customers away from the other banks. But to get money to lend to these customers, the bank will have to pay the wholesale interest rate, which will be high. Thus the bank will lose money by making these loans, and would not be tempted to do so.

Reserve Requirements

The central bank may require that each bank hold deposits at the central bank equal to some fraction of the individual bank's deposits or loans. It may do this even when it does not try to influence the total volume of bank deposits by controlling the volume of deposits with the central bank. If the central bank pays the wholesale money rate on the deposits of other banks with it, then this requirement will have no effect on the banking system. But if the central bank pays a lower rate than the wholesale money rate, this requirement will represent a tax on bank deposits. This tax will mean that banks will pay less than the wholesale rate on their deposits, too. It will cause the economy to revert somewhat to the use of personal and business notes for borrowing and lending.

Limited Reserves

If the central bank establishes reserve requirements in the form of deposits that each bank must carry with the central bank, and sets a rate of interest on these deposits, there will be a natural level of reserves. The higher the reserve requirements and the lower the rate of interest paid on reserves, the larger the tax on deposits, and the more the economy will revert to the use of personal and business notes for borrowing and lending. If, in addition, the central bank sets a maximum limit to the volume of reserves that is lower than the natural level of reserves, it will cause reserves to be worth more to banks than their face value. There is no way for the central bank to set a minimum limit on the volume of reserves other than by changing reserve requirements and the interest rate paid on reserves.

With the quantity of reserves limited to a level below its natural level, reserves take on a value greater than their nominal value. A bank with $1 million on deposit with the central bank might be able to sell its deposit to another bank for $1.5 million. This would increase the effective reserve requirements and reduce the effective rate of interest on reserves so that banks will be satisfied with the amount of reserves allowed by the central bank at the "black market" price. The central bank would have to be careful about accepting new deposits in this situation, since any deposit it accepts results in a windfall gain to the bank making the deposit, equal to the difference between the nominal value of the deposit and the market value of the deposit. The central bank would have to set up a system of rationing for accepting new deposits or for retiring existing deposits. Thus, this would be a very cumbersome system. Since limiting reserves has the same effect on the banking system as increasing reserve requirements or reducing the rate of interest on reserves, but requires rationing of changes in reserves, it is hard to see why this system would be used.

Currency Reserves

If a central bank deposits and currency were both allowed as reserves, if the central bank allowed a bank to increase its deposits with the central bank by depositing currency, and if the central bank limited the quantity of reserves below the natural level, then a very strange situation would be set up. Currency would be worth as much to a bank as deposits with the central bank; in particular, currency would be worth more than its face value to a bank. This means that banks would offer individuals more than face value for currency. An individual making a deposit of currency would have his account credited with the market value of the currency rather than with the face value of the currency. A two-price system would thus be established for all payments: one price for payment by check (the higher price) and one price for payment by currency (the lower price).

This would hardly be a desirable state of affairs. So if currency is to be equivalent to deposits with the central bank for use as reserves, the central bank must refrain from limiting the total supply of reserves to a level below its natural level. The central bank can control reserve requirements and the interest rate paid on reserves, but cannot, unless it wants either rationing or a two-price system, control the supply of reserves.

Since our present banking system allows the use of currency as reserves, and since we do not observe that banks are willing to pay more than face value for currency (in crediting a bank account), it seems likely that the Federal Reserve Board does not set the maximum quantity of reserves below its natural level. In other words, open market operations must be ineffective. If they were effective in controlling the quantity of reserves, then we would observe a two-price system. The only other possibility is that there is a profit opportunity that banks have not been exploiting, in paying more than face value for currency and central bank deposits.

All of these forms of central bank control tend to keep the total volume of banking below its optimal level. They all cause the economy to revert, in part, to the use of personal and business notes for borrowing and lending. Thus they make the financial system less efficient than it would otherwise be. Other than this, these forms of central bank control have no effect on the economy or on the price level.

Monopoly Banking

Even in a world with just one bank, there would be no money supply and the bank would have no significant influence on the real economy or on prices. The bank would not be forced by competition with other banks to offer high interest rates on deposits, but it would be influenced by other financial markets. If it offered very low rates on deposits, it might find that its deposits declined so much that it was more profitable to offer a higher rate and get more deposits. In any case, it is true that such a bank would charge more for transactions, would set higher interest rates on loans and might set lower interest rates on deposits, than a bank in competition with other banks.

It would not, however, be able to cause inflation by bidding up asset prices or by creating deposits that cannot be extinguished. First of all, it would not be allowed to own real assets or common stocks. And second, even if it were allowed to own such assets, it could not create deposits that could not be extinguished. A bank deposit can always be extinguished by being applied to reduction of a bank loan.

The Myth of Aggregate Demand

Those who believe that a central bank can influence the real sector of the economy often say that it does so by affecting aggregate demand for goods and services. In general their argument is that the central bank can make loans easier to get or cheaper, which will expand aggregate demand, and that it can make loans harder to get or more expensive, which will contract aggregate demand. High aggregate demand is supposed to lead to low unemployment but rapid inflation; while low aggregate demand is supposed to lead to high unemployment but stable prices. Sometimes this argument centers on loans that businesses use to buy investment goods, and sometimes it centers on loans that individuals use to buy consumption goods.

What this argument overlooks is the fact that banks must have deposits for all their loans. When a bank allows one person to borrow, it must attract an additional deposit equal to the amount borrowed. When one individual decides to spend more, some other individual must decide to spend less. Borrowing must equal lending; an increase in one must be balanced by an increase in the other. Thus an added demand for consumption goods by one individual must be balanced by a reduced demand for consumption goods by another individual. So aggregate demand is not affected.

Even when the central bank is able to affect the desired balance between consumption and investment, this does not mean that it is thereby able to affect aggregate demand. An increase in desired saving that is balanced by a decrease in desired consumption will leave aggregate demand unchanged. The central bank can increase borrowing only if it increases lending, and it can restrain borrowing only if it restrains lending. Restraining borrowing and lending will cause inefficiencies and misallocation of resources, but it is not clear that it will have any effect on aggregate demand.

The Quantity Theory of Money

In a world where transactions take place by the transfer of loans and deposits, the quantity theory has no place. As I have emphasized above, there is no reasonable definition of the quantity of money in such a world.

The quantity theory has a certain amount of plausibility in a world where the only means of payment is a commodity such as gold. If the supply of gold increases because new gold is found, then it seems fairly reasonable that the prices of other goods would rise relative to the price of gold. The quantity theory also has some plausibility in a world where the government creates currency in massive amounts and spends it for goods and services, as a substitute for direct taxation. However, there is a tendency in such a world for currency to lose its ability to serve as a means of payment. If this happens, then the quantity theory will no longer apply.

As soon as we get to a world where payments are made by transferring deposits and notes, the quantity theory becomes impossible even to formulate. Those who believe in the quantity theory are forced to argue in terms of a world with commodity money or a world where the government hands out massive amounts of currency or bonds, and then transfer their conclusions to an entirely different kind of world.

The Liquidity Preference Theory

In a world where transactions take place by the transfer of loans, deposits, and notes, the liquidity preference theory is just as inappropriate as the quantity theory. This is true whether we have competitive banking or monopoly banking, and whether banks are regulated by a central bank or are completely unregulated.

The general argument is similar to that of the quantity theory. When people have too much "money," they spend it, or they bid up the prices of financial assets, causing interest rates to fall, and stimulating business investment. When people have too little "money," they reduce their spending or sell financial assets, causing interest rates to rise and restraining business investment. Thus too much money increases aggregate demand, and too little money reduces aggregate demand.

But why should people do this? If they have too much money, in either currency or deposits, they can simply pay off their loans. If they have no loans, they can lend their deposits to someone who does, and charge him a little less interest than the bank would charge; he will then use the proceeds to pay off his loans with the bank.

An individual can adjust his portfolio of financial assets by trading with other individuals and by dealing with his bank. If he wants more currency, the bank will give it to him; if he wants less, the bank will take it back. If he wants more demand deposits, the bank will give him a loan (at some interest rate), and if he wants less, the bank will reduce his loans. If the bank will not do these things, other individuals or businesses will.

So transactions that affect portfolio composition are purely financial; they have no impact on the real sector or on the price level.

I am grateful for comments on earlier drafts of the chapter by Myron Scholes, Franco Modigliani, Martin Bailey, James Lorie, John McQuown, Jack Treynor, and Michael Jensen.

References

Friedman, Milton and Schwartz, Anna J. 1969: The definition of money: Net wealth and neutrality as criteria. *Journal of Money, Credit, and Banking*, February, 1–14.

Gurley, John G. and Shaw, Edward S. 1960: *Money in a Theory of Finance*. Washington, DC: The Brookings Institution.

Johnson, Harry G. 1969: Inside money, outside money, income, wealth, and welfare in monetary theory. *Journal of Money, Credit, and Banking*, February, 30–45.

Patinkin, Don 1965: *Money, Interest, and Prices*, 2nd edition. New York: Harper and Row.

Pesek, Boris P. 1968: Comment. *Journal of Political Economy*, July/August, 885–92.

Pesek, Boris P. and Saving, Thomas R. 1967: *Money, Wealth, and Economic Theory*. New York: Macmillan.

Tobin, James 1969: A general equilibrium approach to monetary theory. *Journal of Money, Credit, and Banking*, February 15–29.

Tobin, James 1963: Commercial banks and creators of "money." In Deane Carson (ed.), *Banking and Monetary Studies*, Homewood, Illinois: Richard D. Irwin, Inc. 408–19. Also in Donald D. Hester and James Tobin (eds), *Financial Markets and Economic Activity*, Cowles Foundation Monograph 21. New York: John Wiley & Sons, Inc., 1–11.

Tobin, James 1968: Notes on optimal monetary growth. *Journal of Political Economy*, July/August, 833–59.

Tobin, James and Brainard, William C. 1963: Financial intermediaries and the effectiveness of monetary controls. *American Economic Review*, May, 383–400. Also in Donald D. Hester and James Tobin (eds), *Financial Markets and Economic Activity*, Cowles Foundation Monograph 21. New York: John Wiley & Sons, Inc., 55–93.

Vickrey, William S. 1955: Stability through inflation. In Kenneth K. Kurihara (ed.), *Post-Keynesian Economics*, London: George Allen and Unwin Ltd., 89–122.

Vickrey, William S. 1964: Metastatics and Macroeconomics, New York: Harcourt, Brace & World, Inc.

2

Active and Passive Monetary Policy in a Neoclassical Model

Introduction

Modern macroeconomic theories are customarily classified as either neoclassical or Keynesian. Neoclassical theories are those that assume that most markets are in equilibrium most of the time; in particular, they generally assume that the labor market is always in equilibrium. Keynesian theories are those that assume that many markets are in disequilibrium much of time; in addition to the labor market, they generally assume that financial markets and markets for capital goods are often in disequilibrium. In this chapter, we will be interested in the extent to which a theory assumes that markets are in equilibrium, rather than in the intellectual tradition of the theory, so we will classify theories as "equilibrium theories" or "disequilibrium theories." We will be interested in dynamic theories, which describe the development of prices, stocks, and flows of goods and services over time, rather than in static theories, which describe the impact of events such as a one-time change in tastes, technology, or government policy.

Let us define an equilibrium theory as one in which all markets are in continual equilibrium; in which there are never excess demands or excess supplies of any assets, goods, or services; and in which expectations of future prices and quantities are formed in a rational manner. This last condition is often violated; many theories, for example, assume that individuals maintain expectations of the rates

Reprinted with permission from *The Journal of Finance*, Vol. XXVII, No. 4, September, 1972.

of change of prices in the future that are consistently higher (or lower) than actual past rates of change of prices.

Disequilibrium theories tend to be unsatisfactory because they are inconsistent with the assumptions that individuals act to maximize utility and that firms act to maximize profits. A disequilibrium theory will generally give an individual or firm that is familiar with the theory the ability to make profits from this knowledge, either by trading in financial markets or by operating businesses in real markets. However, the exploitation of these profit opportunities will tend to eliminate them; thus such a theory contains the seeds of its own destruction. A disequilibrium theory is unlikely to be a stable description of the economy for any significant length of time.

Some disequilibrium theories are said to be consistent with maximizing behavior by individuals and firms because of the presence of specific market imperfections, such as transactions costs in securities markets, marketing costs in product markets, and job information costs in labor markets. (For example, see Foley, 1970 and Alchian, 1970.) In most aggregate theories, however, there is no attempt to rationalize their disequilibrium properties, and the departures from equilibrium consistent with these theories are generally too large to be explained by these kinds of market imperfections.

Gordon and Hynes (1970) have made this point specifically for theories that attempt to assign a role to monetary policy in determining unemployment in the labor markets. They note that these theories imply not only that individuals are ignorant, but also that they are unable to learn by experience.

Many dynamic theories make use of a device that was stated formally by Samuelson [1947, p. 263, eq. (11)]. He wrote:

$$\frac{dp}{dt} = H[D(p,\alpha) - S(p)]. \tag{2.1}$$

In this equation, D and S are the demand for and supply of a single commodity, p is its price, α is a shift parameter, and H is a constant representing the speed of adjustment of the price. It says that the price of a commodity rises when there is excess demand and falls when there is excess supply. The instantaneous rate at which the price rises is proportional to the magnitude of the excess demand.

Equation (2.1) is clearly a disequilibrium equation, since it assumes that the demand for the commodity can differ substantially from the supply for an indefinite period of time, especially if the shift parameter is continually changing. Any theory that makes use of a device like equation (2.1), as Gordon and Hynes have pointed out, is a disequilibrium theory.

Many other dynamic theories make use of a similar device, introduced by Cagan (1956), that makes the expected rate of change of a price depend on the lagged past rates of change of the same price. His equation is [1956, p. 37, eq. (5)]:

$$\left(\frac{dE}{dt}\right)_t = \beta(C_t - E_t) \quad \beta \geqslant 0. \tag{2.2}$$

In this equation, C_t and E_t are the actual and expected rates of change of prices at time t and β is a constant that determines the speed of adjustment of expected to actual rates of change of prices. (The rate of change of prices is the time derivative of the log of the price level.)

As Muth (1961) has pointed out, unless the rate of change of prices is changing in a very special (and random) manner, equation (2.2) represents an irrational process for the adjustment of expectations. It implies that E_t can be consistently higher (or lower) than C_t for long periods of time, even when C_t is constant. Thus any theory that uses a device similar to equation (2.2), unless it generates C_t by a particular random process, will be a disequilibrium theory.

Cagan was trying to explain hyperinflation, which may well be a disequilibrium phenomenon. But other writers have used the idea of a lag in expectations to explain a wide variety of economic phenomena. For example, the quantity theory of money, when stated as a dynamic theory, usually makes use of this device: Friedman (1969, p. 41) states flatly, "we know that it takes a long time for people fully to adjust their anticipations to experience," and then proceeds to introduce an expected rate of price change that differs from the actual rate of price change. His desire to do this is understandable, since Cagan points out that a dynamic quantity theory in which the expected and actual rates of price change are equal will give rise to an explosively rising or falling price level. It appears that the quantity theory cannot be stated as a dynamic equilibrium theory.

One of the purposes of this chapter is to develop an aggregate model of the development over time of an economy that includes money and that is in continual equilibrium in the sense described above. Such a model would help in the analysis of the properties of a competitive monetary economy, and would be a logical starting point for the analysis of such phenomena as unemployment and changes in the rate of inflation. Since most Keynesian models of the economy do not pretend to be equilibrium models, let us turn to the neoclassical models of economic growth.

Growth Models

Solow's model of economic growth (1956) has a single commodity that serves as both a production good and a consumption good, and assumes a production function involving both capital and labor, with constant returns to scale and diminishing marginal rates of substitution of capital for labor. He shows that under rather weak conditions, the economy will converge to a steady state growth path in which the stock of capital is growing at the same rate as the population. The equilibrium per-capita stock of capital will be independent of the initial per-capita stock of capital, within limits. He assumes that aggregate consumption is independent of the stock of capital, and that saving is a constant fraction of output, so in the special case in which the population is constant, per-capita wealth does not converge to an equilibrium value, but grows indefinitely. If he had used a more general consumption function, then the growth features of his model would not have been very important, and we could view it as a basic aggregate model of an economy in which all markets are in continual equilibrium.

The Solow model, however, has neither money nor a government sector, so it is not possible to explore the effects of fiscal and monetary policy on the real variables of the economy or on the price level. The first attempts to introduce money into a growth model are made by Tobin (1965) and Johnson (1969). Both Tobin and Johnson assume that money is a liability of the government, that the government controls the quantity of money, that the quantity of money may influence the price level, and that an individual's savings will be allocated between capital and money. They assume that the government does not have any liabilities other than money, so there is no distinction between monetary and fiscal policy in their models. Under these assumptions, they show that government policy does influence the equilibrium value of per-capita capital, and thus the equilibrium wage and the equilibrium level of per-capita output. Neither of these models, however, develops the dynamics of the response of the economy to changes in government policy.

Diamond (1965) develops a dynamic growth model that avoids Solow's assumption that saving is a constant fraction of output by deriving saving behavior from individual utility functions. He introduces interest-bearing government debt, and shows that the effects found by Tobin and Johnson are present when the government's liabilities are bonds rather than money. Diamond's model, then, successfully introduces fiscal policy into a growth model, and shows that the original Tobin and Johnson monetary growth models cannot be regarded as demonstrating anything about the effects of monetary policy as distinct from fiscal policy.

Tobin (1968) then refines his theory, to try to distinguish between the effects of monetary and non-monetary government liabilities, but continues to assume that the government issues only one type of liability. He does introduce dynamics explicitly into his model, but makes the arbitrary assumption that the rate of change of price is equal to the rate of growth of the money supply. He does not even mention the potential for instability in the price level that he noted in his earlier paper (1965).

Sidrauski (1967) is perhaps the first to introduce dynamics explicitly into a monetary growth model. He continues to use a model in which money is the only government liability, but he uses Diamond's device of deriving aggregate saving behavior from individual utility functions, thus avoiding the lack of a steady state in a society with zero population growth. He finds that his model is unstable if he assumes that individuals know the current rate of inflation at all times, so he introduces a lag in expectations similar to that expressed in equation (2.2). Thus his dynamic model is not an equilibrium model.

Foley, Shell, and Sidrauski (1969) develop a dynamic two-sector growth model that has both monetary and non-monetary government liabilities, and thus has room for both fiscal and monetary government policy. They assume, however, that the government uses a mix of fiscal and monetary policy that is consistent with stable prices. They do not explore the possibility of instability if the government should deviate from a policy consistent with stable prices.

Foley and Sidrauski (1970) develop a more general dynamic two-sector growth model that allows the rate of inflation to change over time as a result of changes in government policy. To make their model stable, however, they are forced to introduce a lag in expectations like that in equation (2.2). Thus their model is not an equilibrium model.

Active and Passive Monetary Policy

None of the models mentioned above is the kind of model we are looking for: a stable dynamic growth model that assumes that all markets are in continual equilibrium, that expectations are formed rationally, and that the government can influence the economy through both fiscal and monetary policy. The fact that such a model has not been developed suggests that there is some fundamental difficulty involved. In fact, it appears that there can be no stable dynamic model of the economy that allows the government to use fiscal and monetary policy independently.

Olivera (1970, 1971) suggests a solution to this problem. He shows that a monetary growth model in which expectations are formed rationally and the money supply is given exogenously will be unstable, and shows that if the price level is given exogenously and the money supply is determined endogenously, the model will almost always be stable. A model in which the money supply is given exogenously can be said to allow "active monetary policy," while a model in which the price level is given exogenously can be said to require "passive monetary policy."

Foley, Shell, and Sidrauski are assuming that the government follows a passive monetary policy when they say that it chooses a mix of fiscal and monetary policy that ensures a stable price level. Foley and Sidrauski also consider the case in which the government chooses a policy mix that ensures a stable price level. Both papers show that under these conditions, the economy is stable for a wide variety of initial conditions.

The Olivera model is limited, because it assumes that money is the only type of government liability. So it is not possible to explore the independence of monetary and fiscal policy. The other two models allow the government to issue either bonds or money, but they are unnecessarily complex because they are two-sector models. Let us develop here a simple one-sector monetary growth model that allows the government to issue both bonds and money, but assumes that expectations are always formed rationally.

We will assume constant returns to scale, so all quantities will be written on a per-capita basis. Capital is k, and output is $f(k)$. The real interest rate r is equal to the marginal product of capital, so we have:

$$r = f'(k). \tag{2.3}$$

The rate of inflation π is equal to the fractional rate of change in the price level:

$$\pi = \dot{p}/p. \tag{2.4}$$

We will assume that both the price level and the rate of inflation change continuously over time, and that the expected rate of inflation is always equal to the actual rate of inflation.[1] The nominal interest rate i will then be equal to the real interest rate plus the rate of inflation.

$$i = r + \pi. \tag{2.5}$$

Nominal government liabilities g are divided between bonds b and money m.

$$g = b + m. \tag{2.6}$$

We will assume that the bonds are very short in maturity, so that the nominal value of a bond remains constant while the interest rate varies. We will assume that bonds and capital are perfect substitutes in individuals' asset portfolios, so the nominal interest rate on bonds will be equal to the nominal interest rate on capital. Individuals are allowed to issue bonds, so b is the net quantity of bonds outstanding.

The government will be assumed to follow a constant balanced-budget fiscal policy, so the nominal quantity of government liabilities g does not change over time. The division of government liabilities between bonds and money may change, however.

Per-capita real wealth a, from the point of view of the individual, is the sum of capital and the real quantity of government liabilities.

$$a = k + g/p. \tag{2.7}$$

We will use an aggregate per-capita consumption function $c(a)$ that depends only on wealth. The phenomena that we will be investigating do not depend on the exact functional form of the consumption function. We could include output or disposable income or labor income, real money balances, the interest rate, and the rate of inflation without changing the analysis in any significant way. We will also assume that the population is stable. Thus the rate of change in the supply of capital is simply output minus consumption.

$$\dot{k} = f(k) - c(k + g/p). \tag{2.8}$$

If the price level is constant, this economy will have a steady-state stock of capital defined by:

$$f(k) = c(k + g/p). \tag{2.9}$$

The individual's assets consist of capital, bonds, and money. Capital and bonds are perfect substitutes, so the only decision he has to make is how to divide his wealth between bonds and money. We will assume that money bears no interest. We will write the aggregate per-capita demand for real money balances $L(a,r,\pi)$ as a function of wealth, the real interest rate, and the rate of inflation. When the market for real balances is in equilibrium, we have:

$$m/p = L(k + g/p, r, \pi). \tag{2.10}$$

The rate of consumption will be assumed to increase with wealth.

$$\frac{\partial c}{\partial a} > 0. \tag{2.11}$$

The elasticity of the demand for money with respect to wealth will be assumed to be between zero and one.[2] An increment to wealth is divided between money and other assets in a ratio less than the existing ratio of money to other assets.

$$0 < \frac{\partial L}{\partial a} < \frac{L}{a}. \tag{2.12}$$

An increase in either r or π means an increase in the nominal interest rate, and thus a shift of wealth from money to capital or bonds.

$$\frac{\partial L}{\partial r} < 0, \qquad \frac{\partial L}{\partial \pi} < 0. \tag{2.13}$$

If we assume that the money supply is given exogenously, and that the price level is determined endogenously, then this economy is globally unstable. There are steady-state paths for the economy, in

which the money supply, the price level, and the stock of capital
are constant, but if the economy is disturbed from such a steady-
state path, or if it starts from a position not on a steady-state path,
the price level will eventually either rise at a continually accelerating
rate or fall at a continually accelerating rate.

Suppose, for example, that the economy is on a steady-state path
with all variables constant in time, and that there is a shift in demand
that requires a positive rate of inflation to satisfy equation (2.10).
Then the price level will start to rise, which will cause the real money
supply to fall faster than the demand, which will accelerate the rate
of inflation. Meanwhile, the decline in real wealth will cause a decline
in consumption, an increase in the capital stock, and a decline in
the interest rate. Both the increase in the capital stock and the decline
in the interest rate will increase the demand for money, causing π
to increase still faster to keep the demand for money equal to the
supply. These changes will continue in the same direction without
limit. Eventually the real value of government liabilities will become
negligible relative to the capital stock, and the capital stock will
gradually approach a maximum value. But the price level will
continue to accelerate upwards.

Similarly, if there is a shift in demand that gives π a negative value
initially, the price level will fall at an accelerating rate. In this case, the
increase in the real value of government liabilities will cause capital to
be consumed continuously, and will cause a continuing increase in the
real interest rate. While the rate of deflation can never be greater than
the real interest rate, the real interest rate is increasing continuously,
so the rate of deflation can increase continuously as well.

It can be shown that if the money supply is held constant, any
initial values of p and k other than steady-state values will lead
eventually to runaway inflation or runaway deflation. So the system
is globally unstable.

On the other hand, suppose that we assume that the time path
of the price level is given exogenously, and that the money supply is
determined endogenously. Then there is no possible source of instability
in the economy. Equations (2.8) and (2.10) will determine the time
path of the capital stock and the money supply in a straightforward
manner. If the price level increases over time, the capital stock will
increase, but the changes that occur will be orderly and stable.

Taking the money supply as exogenous is unsatisfactory for reasons
other than the instability that results. Note that an increase in the
nominal money supply in equation (2.10) will be consistent with an

accelerating deflation, rather than with an increase in the price level. Thus equation (2.10) is completely inconsistent with the usual economic logic describing the effects of monetary policy on the economy.

Also, it is not even clear how an active monetary policy can be implemented in this economy. A passive monetary policy can be implemented easily: the government simply agrees to exchange money for bonds, or bonds for money, on demand. This will not cause the public to exchange all of its bonds for money because money bears no interest. The amount of money that the public will choose to hold is given by equation (2.10).

Since bonds are very short-term instruments, the public in effect has a savings account with the government. The government can control the money supply only by refusing to accept a deposit of money from the public, or by refusing to redeem its bonds in money. Both of these acts are inconsistent with continual equilibrium in the money and bond markets. Note that the government cannot increase the money supply simply by making transfer payments in money, because the public will react to this by returning the money to the government in exchange for bonds, unless such exchanges are prohibited.

There is, of course, an active monetary policy that would respond to all disturbances in the economy in a way that is consistent with price stability. But the required policy is an odd one and is a difficult one to follow. When inflation appears, the money supply must first be increased and must later be decreased. If the required policy is not followed exactly, the inflation will either accelerate or turn into an accelerating deflation. A constant money supply is not consistent with price stability, nor is a money supply growing at a constant rate. There is no simple rule of thumb for the management of the money supply that is consistent with price stability.

These features continue to hold if we allow the government to have an active fiscal policy. We can allow the government to buy goods either for public consumption or for investment, and we can allow it to finance its purchases through either taxes or an increase in outstanding government liabilities. These choices can be made arbitrarily, but once they are made, there is no opportunity for an active monetary policy. The model continues to give an accelerating inflation or deflation if the money supply is chosen exogenously; it continues to have the property that an increase in the rate of growth of the money supply is associated with more rapid deflation rather than more rapid inflation ; and it continues to require that the government destroy equilibrium in the money and bond markets in order to implement its monetary policy.[3]

Also, while the model outlined above, with or without added features, has an algebraic solution, it is very difficult to imagine an economic process that will cause changes in the money supply, or in the rate of growth of the money supply, to lead to changes in the rate of inflation, if we continue to insist on continual equilibrium in all markets. The usual argument is that an increase in the money supply causes individuals to bid up the prices of long-term bonds, causing an increase in the price level or the rate of inflation, and causing firms to borrow for investment and thus to bid up the prices of investment goods. This model makes it clear that this "quantity theory" argument is inconsistent with dynamic equilibrium. Individuals can reduce their money holdings by exchanging them for bonds. And since the bonds are short-term instruments, such an exchange will have no effect on the interest rate. There is no reason for individuals to try to bid up the prices of consumer goods.

It is clear that the government has no direct control over the interest rate in this model, so it cannot implement monetary policy by changing the interest rate. The real rate is equal to the marginal product of capital, which is determined by the capital stock. The nominal rate is equal to the real rate plus the rate of inflation, and the government certainly has no direct control over the rate of inflation. Thus there is no way for the government to control the nominal interest rate.

This lack of a mechanism by which monetary policy can affect the price level has been pointed out by others. For example, Chow (1970), in a review of Friedman's *The Optimum Quantity of Money and Other Essays*, points out that Friedman has nowhere given an adequate explanation of the mechanism that links the quantity of money with other economic variables. He also points out that Friedman has never explicitly formulated the dynamics of the quantity theory of money.

It has been suggested that one simple way out of these difficulties is to introduce disequilibrium only in the labor market, by assuming a nominal wage rate that is inflexible downward. Unfortunately, this will not help. If price deflation causes unemployment, then output will fall, and the rate of consumption of capital will increase. This will only accelerate the deflation in the model described above. And the case of runaway inflation will not be affected at all by a wage rate that is inflexible downward. Even if the possibility of unemployment would make the system mathematically stable, we would still have the problem of describing an economic process by which an increase in the rate of growth of the money supply can lead to deflation, as required by the model.

To make the model mathematically stable, given an exogenous money supply, it is necessary to introduce consistent disequilibrium in the goods market or in the bond and money markets, or to assume consistent stupidity in the form of a lag in expectations. These assumptions are very hard to accept, because they imply profit opportunities for firms and individuals that are not exploited.

Previous writers on monetary growth models have emphasized the question of whether monetary policy can have short-run or long-run effects on the real sector, or whether it affects only the price level. If the simple model described above could be interpreted as allowing active monetary policy, it would say that monetary policy is not neutral, because it affects the capital stock, output, and consumption in both the short run and the long run. But there does not appear to be any way to interpret the model as allowing the money supply to be determined exogenously, so it seems to say that monetary policy can affect neither the real sector nor the price level.

Thus it appears that in a neoclassical model in which individuals act to maximize utility and firms act to maximize profits, there is no room for an active monetary policy that determines the money supply exogenously. The only consistent monetary policy is a passive one, in which the price level is taken as exogenous, and the money supply is determined endogenously.

Passive Monetary Policy and the Price Level

The idea of an exogenous price level is unusual and is simply an indication that the model is incomplete. If monetary policy does not determine the price level, what does?

In the simple model described above, there are not many variables that could influence the price level. The capital stock is one variable, and it determines output and the real interest rate. The real stock of government liabilities is another variable, and it (together with the capital stock) determines consumption. To determine the price level endogenously, we might add an equation that expresses the rate of inflation as a function of the capital stock and the real stock of government liabilities. The dependent variable is the rate of inflation rather than the price level itself, so that the price level will change in a continuous manner over time.[4]

$$\pi = h(k, g/p). \tag{2.14}$$

There is a wide variety of functions h that can be chosen so that the price level will not go into accelerating inflation or deflation. In particular, any function that is bounded both above and below will be consistent with stability.

In a more general model, there would be other variables that might influence the price level, such as the rate of government expenditure, and the size of the government's budget deficit. In a multi-sector model, discoveries of natural resources or inventions might affect the price level. In a model allowing unemployment, the level of unemployment might affect the price level. Thus it is perfectly possible to model the inflations associated with wars and discoveries of gold, and the deflations associated with rapid technological progress and depressions, without assuming an active monetary policy.

In any more general model of dynamic equilibrium that includes money and a continuous price level along the lines suggested by the model outlined above, there is likely to be an association between the money stock and the price level, even though both variables may be taken as endogenous to the model. An increase in prices causes an increase in the nominal values of wealth, output, disposable income, and consumption, so the demand for money will increase when the price level increases. If monetary policy is passive, the supply of money will increase with the demand. Thus a correlation between the money stock and the price level need not be interpreted as Friedman and Schwartz (1963) interpret it as evidence of the effectiveness of an active monetary policy. Krooss (1964) claims that the more natural interpretation of the evidence presented by Friedman and Schwartz, at least in many cases, is that the money supply is a passive rather than an active variable.

Some writers have said that if the government allows the supply of money to expand freely to meet the demand, there will be no equilibrium price level, and prices will increase continuously. But the model outlined above suggests that there is not only one, but many equilibrium price levels consistent with a passive monetary policy. The model does not suggest any mechanism that would cause a passive monetary policy to lead to unbounded inflation.

Banking and Inside Money

The model we have described assumes that there are two kinds of financial assets: bonds and money. In our description of the model, we said that the money was a liability of the government, while the bonds were issued by individuals as well as by the government. The model does not change in any way, however, if we assume that the money is issued by a banking sector rather than by the government and thus is "inside money" as characterized by Gurley and Shaw (1960).

We can assume that all money is inside money, which takes the form of both demand deposits (which bear no interest) and currency. The currency would then be in the form of bank notes and privately minted coins. We can assume that a bank is required to hold government bonds equal to 100 percent of the value of its demand deposits and currency outstanding. Now all government liabilities will be in the form of bonds.

The analysis made in previous sections is not changed in any way by these assumptions. The production and consumption functions remain the same, and the demand function for money is unchanged. If a passive monetary policy is adopted, the banks can be allowed to create money freely to satisfy the demand. If the public has more money than it wants, it will simply give it to the banks in exchange for government bonds or private bonds (time deposits) issued by the banks. If the public has too little money, it will exchange government or private bonds for bank money. There will be nothing to cause pressure of any kind on the price level by the use of a passive monetary policy.

An active monetary policy, however, is so inconsistent with equilibrium that it is difficult to see how it could be implemented in an inside money economy. Would the government assign money quotas to individual banks? Would a bank lose the quota associated with a deposit that is transferred to another bank? Would banks refuse to exchange money for bonds when this would mean exceeding their quotas?

To try to salvage the notion of active monetary policy under dynamic equilibrium, let us turn to an economy with both outside money and inside money, and let us assume that the government controls the supply of outside money. Let us assume that the outside money is used as currency, and that the bank is required to hold outside money equal to a certain percentage of the value of its demand deposits, and is required to hold government bonds equal to the remainder of the value of its demand deposits.

We now have all the same problems that we had in previous models. The only way the government can control the supply of outside money is to refuse to exchange money and bonds freely, which implies lack of equilibrium in the money and bond markets. If there is too much outside money outstanding, as Gramley and Chase (1965) have pointed out, the public will not hold it, so it will become unwanted free reserves held by the banks. This is again inconsistent with equilibrium in the outside money market. Eventually, the banks will refuse to accept outside money in exchange for bonds or time deposits, and it will tend to lose its status as a means of payment. Similarly, if there is too little outside money outstanding, the banks will have to ration their demand deposits, and will be reluctant to exchange outside money for bonds, time deposits, or demand deposits. Since both inside and outside money will be in short supply, individuals will be reluctant to use it in paying for goods and services, and will tend to use some form of credit instead. Again, money will tend to lose its status as a means of payment.

Note that even in a system with both inside and outside money, there is no mechanism for changes in the money supply to cause changes in the price level. Nor is there any way consistent with market equilibrium for the banks to issue more or less money than the public wants to hold. In the model discussed here, this is particularly easy to see, since the banks do not make loans. They cannot try to expand the money supply by making loans at low interest rates, and they cannot try to expand the money supply by buying long-term government bonds.

Even in an equilibrium model in which the banks do hold loans and long-term bonds, however, the money supply is still not under the control of the banks or the government. If a bank issues money to make a loan to one person, and that money is more than the public wants to hold at equilibrium interest rates, then it will simply be used to pay off another loan, at the same bank or at another bank. And if a bank issues extra money to buy long-term government bonds, that money will simply be deposited in a time deposit, or used to buy government bonds at the next auction. So long as the public can exchange money for interest-bearing assets and liabilities, there is no reason to believe that the government's or the banks' attempts to control the money supply will result in changes in aggregate consumption, aggregate income, or the price level in an equilibrium model.

Policy Implications

This analysis raises the question of whether monetary policy as practiced in the United States is truly active or not. Since the Federal Reserve tends to rely heavily on "net free reserves" in determining its policy, it is possible that it acts primarily in a passive mode, absorbing reserves when net free reserves get too large. The fact that it allows banks to borrow reserves at all tends to make its control over the money supply more passive than active. While many writers have acknowledged these slippages, they have maintained that Federal Reserve policy does have some independent effect on the economy. The fact that any active monetary policy at all may be inconsistent with equilibrium, however, makes one wonder whether Federal Reserve policy has any influence on the economy at all.

The analysis also raises the question of what would happen if the government adopted an openly passive monetary policy. What if the government abolished interest rate ceilings and reserve requirements and offered to exchange currency and reserves freely for government bonds? What if it abandoned attempts to control entry into banking and the terms on which banks can accept deposits? Would there be widespread bank failures? Would there be an accelerating inflation? Would the economy become less stable?

I have given a set of possible answers to these questions in chapter 1. The model discussed here suggests that a passive monetary policy would not introduce any instability into an economy that is continually in equilibrium. I hope that other writers will attempt to show what will happen in their models if a passive monetary policy is adopted. It seems so elementary a question that it is surprising how little attention it has received.

Conclusions

We have explored the properties of a neoclassical model similar to those used by growth theorists, including both money and bonds, with a consumption function that depends on wealth. We have assumed that all markets are continually in equilibrium, that expectations are formed rationally, and that the price level moves continuously over time. We have compared an active monetary policy, as represented by an exogenous money stock and an endogenous rate of inflation, with a passive monetary policy, as represented by an exogenous rate of inflation and an endogenous money stock.

We have found that active monetary policy makes little economic sense in this model. There is no way for the government to implement an active monetary policy that is consistent with continual equilibrium in the money and bond markets. If there were a way to implement an active monetary policy, it would work perversely, with an increase in the money stock being associated with a decrease in the rate of inflation. In addition, the price level would be unstable, and the economy would eventually go into accelerating inflation or deflation.

We have found that passive monetary policy is always consistent with stability in this model and requires no sacrifice of its equilibrium properties.

We have explored a number of possible changes in the model, including changes in the form of the consumption function, the introduction of inflexible wages, and the introduction of a banking sector. None of these changes appears to make active monetary policy consistent with dynamic equilibrium.

These conclusions cast doubt on the stability of the parameters of models that include active monetary policy by allowing markets to be out of equilibrium or by allowing expectations to be formed irrationally. If individuals and firms knew the properties of these models and acted to maximize utility and profits, then the models would stop being valid.

These results suggest that the properties of models that assume passive monetary policy need a great deal more study.

Notes

1 If the price level can jump discontinuously from one level to another, then the analysis becomes much more complex. It becomes necessary to distinguish between anticipated changes in the money supply and in the price level. There is no longer a unique correspondence between paths for the price level (given an initial price level) and paths for the money supply. There will be many paths for the price level consistent with any given path for the money supply. The overall conclusions of that analysis are similar to those in this chapter.

2 This assumption makes the nature of the instability very simple in a model that assumes the money supply is given exogenously. Allowing the wealth elasticity of the demand for money to be one or greater will only change the nature of the instability.

3 A rather thorough analysis of the instability of models in which the money supply is chosen exogenously is given by Burmeister and Dobell (1970, pp. 156–201). They conclude that changing the structure of the model while preserving its equilibrium does not eliminate the instability.

4 In a model in which the price level can change discontinuously, the dependent variable can be taken to be the price level rather than the rate of inflation.

References

Alchian, Armen A. 1970: Information costs, pricing, and resource unemployment. In Edmund S. Phelps (ed.), *Microeconomic Foundations of Employment and Inflation Theory*. New York: Norton, 27–52.

Burmeister, Edwin and Dobell, A. Rodney 1970: *Mathematical Theories of Economic Growth*, New York: Macmillan.

Cagan, Philip 1956: The monetary dynamics of hyperinflation. In Milton Friedman (ed.), *Studies in the Quantity Theory of Money*, Chicago: University of Chicago Press, 23–117.

Chow, Gregory C. 1970: Friedman on money. *Journal of Finance*, 25, 687–9.

Diamond, Peter A. 1965: National debt in a neoclassical growth model. *American Economic Review*, 55, 1125–50.

Gordon, Donald F. and Hynes, Allan 1970: On the theory of price dynamics. In Edmund S. Phelps (ed.), *Microeconomic Foundations of Employment and Inflation Theory*, New York: Norton, 369–93.

Foley, Duncan K. 1970: Economic equilibrium with costly marketing. *Journal of Economic Theory 2*, September, 276–91.

Foley, Duncan K. and Sidrauski, Miguel 1970: Portfolio choice, investment, and growth. *American Economic Review*, 60, 44–63.

Foley, Duncan K., Shell, Karl and Sidrauski, Miguel 1969: Optimal fiscal and monetary policy and economic growth. *Journal of Political Economy*, 77, 698–719.

Friedman, Milton 1969: The optimum quantity of money. In *The Optimum Quantity of Money and Other Essays*, Chicago: Aldine, 1–50.

Friedman, Milton and Schwartz, Anna J. 1963: *A Monetary History of the United States, 1867–1960*. Princeton, NJ: National Bureau of Economic Research.

Gramley, Lyle E. and Chase, Samuel B. 1965: Time deposits in monetary analysis. *Federal Reserve Bulletin*, October, 1380–1404.

Gurley, John G. and Shaw, Edward S. 1960: *Money in a Theory of Finance*. Washington: The Brookings Institution.

Johnson, Harry G. 1969: Money in a neoclassical one-sector growth model. In *Essays in Monetary Economics*, Cambridge, Mass.: Harvard University Press, 143–78.

Krooss, Herman E. 1964: Monetary history and monetary policy: a review article. *Journal of Finance*, 19, 662–7.

Muth, John 1961: Rational expectations and the theory of price movements. *Econometrica* 29, 315–35.

Olivera, Julio H. 1970: On passive money. *Journal of Political Economy*, 78, 805–14.

Olivera, Julio H. 1971: A note on passive money, inflation, and economic growth. *Journal of Money, Credit, and Banking*, 3, 137–44.

Samuelson, Paul A. 1947: *Foundations of Economic Analysis*, Cambridge, Mass.: Harvard University Press.

Sidrauski, Miguel 1967: Rational choice and patterns of growth in a monetary economy. *American Economic Review*, 57, 534–44.

Solow, Robert 1956: A contribution to the theory of economic growth. *Quarterly Journal of Economics*, 70, 65–94.

Tobin, James 1965: Money and economic growth. *Econometrica*, 33, 671–84.

Tobin, James 1968: Notes on optimal monetary growth. *Journal of Political Economy*, 76, 833–59.

3

Rational Economic Behavior and the Balance of Payments

Introduction

This chapter will attempt to explore the implications, for the theory of international trade and the balance of payments, of assuming that individuals behave rationally in the light of all the information available to them. Theories that do not assume that individuals behave rationally are not very satisfactory, because they usually imply that anyone who knows the theory can make money by exploiting the irrationalities of the other individuals. In the process, the person who knows the theory will educate the others, they will stop behaving irrationally (or will become so poor that they stop having an impact on the economy), and the theory will no longer hold.

Rational behavior implies, among other things, that all unemployment is voluntary (or frictional). There is always a wage level at which rational employers would be willing to hire; if individuals choose not to work at the wage levels implied by the supply of and demand for their skills, then they may be acting rationally, but they are not involuntarily unemployed. On the other hand, if individuals are unemployed for long periods of time because they think the equilibrium wage for their skills is higher than it is, then they will be acting irrationally.

Because I believe that Keynesian unemployment is inconsistent with rational behavior on the part of employers and employees, the analysis in this chapter will be in the context of what is sometimes called a neoclassical model. The labor, goods, and capital markets will all be assumed to be in continuous flow and stock equilibrium.

Rational behavior also means that expectations are formed in a sensible manner. For example, the use of "adaptive expectations"

40

is not generally a good way to revise one's expectations.[1] Rational expectations means at least that the expectation of an uncertain variable should always be equal to the expected value of the distribution of possible values of the variable.[2] In a model containing no uncertainty, rational expectations implies perfect foresight.[3]

Rational economic behavior is consistent with the existence of finite costs of acquiring information, changing jobs, shifting capital from one use to another, or transporting goods from one location to another. We are interested simply in a theory that assumes that individuals and firms behave rationally in the light of all that they know at a given point in time, and that they revise their behavior appropriately as they get new information. Many "disequilibrium" theories justify assuming that excess demand or excess supply may persist in a market by calling on information, adjustment, or transaction costs. They do not generally include such costs explicitly, however, and the resulting models are usually not consistent with the assumption that individuals behave rationally in the light of these costs.[4]

International General Equilibrium Without Money

Let us consider a group of countries as a single economic system. We will assume that government fiscal and tariff policies are given in each country. These policies may include domestic taxes and transfers; taxes or subsidies on the flow of goods, services, or factors of production into or out of a country; and taxes or subsidies on domestic holdings of foreign assets or foreign holdings of domestic assets. It does not add much generality to assume that a government may impose quotas on international flows, or that a government may periodically expropriate domestic assets held by foreigners.

We will assume initial stocks of capital goods within each country, and an allocation of ownership of goods and securities among residents of the different countries such that each individual is happy with the composition of her wealth portfolio in the light of government fiscal and tariff policies.

Under various sets of assumptions, including a set of assumptions generally identified with "perfect competition," there will be a unique equilibrium for the international economy at each point in time.[5] In the absence of uncertainty, the dynamic behavior of the system will be uniquely determined. There will be a unique path of relative prices, consumption decisions by individuals, and production decisions by firms such that every market is continuously cleared and every individual is maximizing expected utility. If output for a given pattern of investment is uncertain, or if the parameters of individuals' utility functions are uncertain, then the dynamic behavior of the system will be stochastic, but it will be completely determined by the exogenous random variables in the production or utility functions.

This is true even though there are frictions, adjustment costs, and information costs that individuals and firms must take into account. It is true even though some industries may contain a small number of large firms, so that prices are determined by a "game" whose outcome is uncertain. And it is true even if unions have monopoly power that they use to raise the real wage for their members, even though this means keeping some of their members unemployed.

The path of the international economy is determined entirely by real factors. If it is possible to talk about price levels, fixed exchange rates, or devaluation in a system like this at all, it is clear that devaluation can have no real effects. At most, it can affect the nominal price levels in various countries. Since the assumption of rational economic behavior implies the absence of "money illusion," changes in nominal price levels in various countries, in a world without money, can have no real effects.[6]

Thus neither the "elasticities" approach nor the "absorption" approach to devaluation makes sense in a model that assumes rational behavior and does not include money.[7] One cannot say that devaluation will have any effect on a country's exports, imports, or terms of trade.

The Balance of Trade

We will assume that any country's securities or capital may be owned by residents of any other country. Since private securities are just ownership claims on capital, there is no meaningful distinction between foreign ownership of securities and foreign ownership of capital.

The movement of securities from one country to another is not the same as the movement of physical capital from one country to another, although both are sometimes lumped under the term "investment." Even if we assume that physical capital cannot be moved between countries, securities can flow between countries in exchange for goods or other securities.

If the residents of country A exchange securities for goods produced in country B, then according to the usual terminology, there has been a flow of capital into A. The flow of securities from A to B is a flow of capital from B to A. And it is true whether the securities that flow from A to B are government securities of A, government securities of B, ownership claims on capital in A, or ownership claims on capital in B.[8]

In this kind of a model, it does not make sense to say that capital flows from one country to another because of interest rate differentials or differentials in the expected rates of return on risky securities.[9] An owner of physical capital may transfer it from one country to another because of differences in the real return to capital in the two countries, and it may take time to eliminate such differences, because of costs of transporting capital and because changes in production conditions keep creating such differences anew. But the costs of trading securities are generally very low, so it is not possible for differences in the returns to securities that imply an incentive for everyone to switch from one security to the other to exist. Changes in security prices and interest rates will eliminate such differences immediately.[10]

The residents of a country will choose portfolios of high-risk and low-risk assets that maximize expected utility. If an individual holds several different securities that are essentially riskless, then the after-tax real returns to her on all of them must be the same. Differences in nominal interest rates between countries can exist only because of differences between nominal and real rates of return, differences in tax status, and differences in such other factors as the likelihood of devaluation or expropriation. None of these factors creates any incentive for flows of securities between countries.

In maximizing expected utility, an individual will generally try to hold a diversified portfolio. A resident of country A will want to hold some of country B's securities, and a resident of country B will want to hold some of country A's securities. So they will swap. But this will not result in any net flow of securities or capital. The value of the securities that A gives to B will be equal to the value of the securities that B gives to A.

A country can have either a positive or a negative balance of trade indefinitely. If it is a net lender, then it may have a continuous negative balance of trade representing earnings on its securities. If it is a net borrower, it may have a continuous positive balance of trade representing interest, dividends, and other earnings paid to foreign holders of its securities. The wealthier country will tend to have a negative balance of trade, and the poorer country will tend to have a positive balance of trade. If anything, a negative balance of trade seems more desirable than a positive balance of trade, because it represents holdings of foreign assets.

In the short run, of course, the balance of trade can shift between negative and positive periodically because of changes in the flows of securities. A country that is accumulating foreign securities or capital may have a positive balance of trade while it exports goods in exchange for securities. Later its balance of trade may turn negative as its earnings on its foreign holdings come to exceed its rate of accumulation of securities. Or a country that is a substantial net lender may decide to accumulate more wealth, and may become a net exporter if its rate of accumulation exceeds the earnings on its existing holdings.

In other words, the major factors determining the balance of trade have little to do with foreign exchange reserves or exchange rates. And as we shall see, the direction and magnitude of the balance of trade have little to do with the factors determining the balance of payments.

General Equilibrium with Money

Let us now assume that each country adopts an arbitrary unit of account, expresses all prices in terms of that unit of account, and issues currency expressed in the same unit. Interest and dividend rates within a country will be expressed in terms of that country's unit of account.

Securities that are held in more than one country may trade in each country's currency. For example, Japanese securities held by both Japanese and US residents may have quoted prices in both yen and dollars.

The exchange rate between two countries will be the rate at which the currency of one country may be exchanged for the currency of the other country. Generally there will be a "spread" in the exchange rate, so that the exchange rate for exchanges in one direction will differ slightly from the exchange rate for exchanges in the other direction. Alternatively, there may be a single exchange rate, and a separate transaction charge may be made. The transaction charge will tend to be higher in percentage terms for small transactions at the retail level than for large transactions at the wholesale level.

Each good in each country will now have a nominal price in that country's unit of account, as well as a relative price with respect to each other good. Nominal prices of goods in a country may rise or fall at varying rates, depending on the strength of inflationary or deflationary pressures within that country.[11]

Each individual will decide how she wants to divide her wealth between various securities and currencies on the basis of the known or expected returns on those securities and on the basis of the covariances between the returns on each pair of securities or currencies. Since each country will have securities that are almost as safe as currency and that pay interest at current short-term rates, the short-term nominal interest rate will be an important factor in the demand for money within a country.

The higher the short-term nominal interest rate, the less money an individual will want to hold, other things being equal, and the more effort she will spend economizing on her money balances. When interest rates are high, she will make frequent exchanges between money and short-term interest-bearing securities, to minimize her lost interest.

Similarly, when interest rates are high, firms may have to spend more economizing on their money balances. With a banking system like the one that exists in the United States, most large firms may receive almost the equivalent of interest at full short-term rates on their demand deposits, since the banks reduce the interest rates on their loans to firms by an amount equivalent to the interest on deposits. So the effects of interest rates on the demand for money by firms may be more modest than the effect of interest rates on the demand for money by individuals.

In any case, the cost of economizing on money balances and the influence of the nominal short-term interest rate on the demand for money within a country means that the real aspects of a monetary economy are not independent of its nominal aspects. To specify the state of an international monetary economy, one needs to know the nominal short-term interest rate in each country, and possibly expected future short-term interest rates as well.

But that's all. Assuming that all individuals behave rationally in the light of the information available to them, the supply of real balances must always equal the demand, either because the government supplies passively whatever balances the private sector demands, or because the nominal price level and nominal interest rate adjust so that the supply of nominal balances fixed by the government is accepted by the private sector.

The question of how monetary policy affects a national monetary economy in which everyone acts rationally has not been settled.[12] If the government increases the money stock through a purchase of private capital, there are a number of changes consistent with a larger nominal money stock. The price level may increase abruptly, with the nominal interest rate remaining unchanged, and the rate of inflation returning to its original level after the jump in the price level. Or the price level may remain unchanged, and the nominal interest rate and rate of inflation may *fall* to levels that make the demand for real balances equal to the new level of real balances. Or there may be any of a number of combinations of a jump in the price level, the nominal interest rate, and the rate of inflation that make the demand for money equal to the supply. Rational behavior means that the change in the nominal interest rate will be approximately equal to the change in the rate of inflation, since the change in the real rate due to a change in the cost of economizing on money balances will normally be small.

If we knew how to describe the dynamic process governing the evolution of the short-term interest rate, then we would know how to determine the path of a national or international monetary economy over time. But we don't know yet how to describe that process.[13]

The "monetary approach" to balance of payments theory is rather primitive in its development.[14] Often those who use this approach ignore the existence of securities, and assume that when the money supply is increased within a country, the residents of the country can reduce their balances only by buying domestic or foreign commodities. The introduction of securities completely changes the predictions of their theories. Others include securities, but create static models that cannot be generalized into dynamic models that assume rational economic behavior.

Floating Exchange Rates

A group of countries may choose to do nothing about their exchange rates, and the system should operate smoothly. The changes in exchange rates will be determined primarily by the differences in the rates of inflation in different countries. If national monetary policies influence these rates of inflation, they will influence the exchange rates too.

The principal disadvantage of flexible exchange rates is simply that in order to know the price of a foreign commodity or service, one needs to know the current exchange rate. There is a cost of keeping buyers and sellers informed about changes in price due to changes in exchange rates. The cost does not seem very large, however, since exchange rates can be published in the daily papers.

The uncertainty in the future exchange rate is sometimes said to be a disadvantage, but it is hard to create a set of assumptions that make this true. If a United States manufacturer orders Swiss machinery to be delivered and paid for in three months for a given number of Swiss francs, then the future dollar price is uncertain. But the current dollar price is known. The manufacturer need only convert dollars to Swiss francs and buy a Swiss commercial bill for the desired amount that matures in three months. This would seem to provide as much certainty as anyone might want.

Some theorists claim that floating exchange rates make domestic fiscal policy ineffective.[15] But this is usually in the context of a Keynesian model that assumes that there is unemployment due to irrational behavior on the part of employers and employees.

Fixed Exchange Rates Through Taxation

Any country can try to force its exchange rate with another country to follow a certain path. It can choose any path, but a common choice is to keep the exchange rate constant except for periodic devaluation or revaluation. It is also common to try to keep the exchange rate within a certain band around the chosen path, rather than try to keep it exactly on the path.

One way that a country can try to control its exchange rate is through its tax and related fiscal policies. It can make changes in the taxes on imports or exports, on export industries or import competing industries, or even on purely domestic industries. These changes will in general affect all of the variables of the international economy: the composition of imports and exports, the balance of trade, and the pattern of domestic and foreign investment.

At the moment, we are assuming that the only tool used to influence exchange rates is tax policy. Thus the balance of payments will be identically zero. In this world, tax policy will have no affect on the balance of payments, because currency exchange is handled entirely by the private sector.

For example, suppose a country imposes a 10 percent import tax and a 10 percent export subsidy on all goods and services. It is likely that the value of its currency will fall, perhaps by approximately 10 percent. The balance of trade may change, but the direction of the change is not clear. Any change in the trade balance must be offset by an equal change in the balance of capital flows.

The big disadvantage of this method of fixing exchange rates, of course, is the fact that it introduces distortions into the pattern of world trade and investment that will normally reduce the potential welfare of the world's population.[16] In particular cases, these distortions may offset existing distortions, and increase potential world welfare. Normally, however, they will make things worse. Eventually, when the distortions become severe enough, the country may eliminate many of them all at once and thus cause a sudden devaluation or upward revaluation.

The cost of the distortions introduced by using taxes to control exchange rates is not borne only by the country that imposes the taxes. If other countries do not retaliate, then a country may even increase its potential welfare at the expense of other countries. Even if they do retaliate in such a way that everyone bears part of the cost, the cost is shared. As we shall see, the cost of controlling exchange rates through intervention is borne entirely by the country that intervenes. Thus the use of taxes may be more acceptable politically. In addition, selective taxes will be favored by the industries that will benefit at the expense of individual consumers or competing foreign industries.

Fixed Exchange Rates Through Intervention

The other major way of controlling exchange rates is by intervening directly in the currency exchange market. The government of a country can offer to exchange the two currencies at a fixed rate. The exchange rate at which it will buy its own currency will generally differ from the exchange rate at which it will sell its own currency, however. A government would even be able to fix the exchange rate between two foreign currencies if it wished.

Normally, the pressure to exchange currencies will be in only one direction at a given point in time. If inflationary pressures are higher in the United States than in Britain, the British government will be asked to give pounds for dollars. It can print the pounds it needs, or it can issue government debt to get the pounds it needs, or it can get the pounds through taxation. It will accumulate dollars, which it will normally use to buy dollar-denominated US securities. Its holdings of US securities will increase.

If the inflationary pressure is in Britain, then the process is reversed. The government will sell its US securities for dollars, and will issue the dollars in exchange for pounds. If it runs out of US securities, it may be able to borrow from the US government or in the private capital markets. Since it can pledge its own securities with large coverage as collateral for such loans, it should not have any trouble borrowing dollars. For example, it might pledge $200 million in British government securities as collateral for a $100 million US loan. Then even a substantial devaluation of the pound would leave the US with adequate collateral.

This process should be quite effective in fixing exchange rates. It should force the actual rates of inflation to be comparable in the two countries. The cost of the operation would be related to the volume of intervention necessary. The government would lose the transaction costs on all of the exchanges it participates in.

The fact that the government may be forced to hold US securities is not an additional cost, unless the interest rates on the two countries' securities are distorted by differential tax rates. If both US and British securities are held in substantial quantities in Britain, then rational investors will arbitrage the rates until they are equivalent. (The nominal rates may differ in equilibrium, because the likelihood of devaluation is greater for one country than for the other. This difference in rates will be just sufficient to compensate the holders for the differential chance of devaluation.)

Is there any gain from using fixed exchange rates, other than avoiding the cost of flexible exchange rates? It seems unlikely. The only real effect that exchange rate policy can have in a world of rational economic behavior is on the cost of economizing on money balances. If exchange rate policy can be used to make a country's average rate of inflation or the world's average rate of inflation lower than it would otherwise be, then there will be a small real gain. It does not seem likely that this gain will be large enough to offset the cost of maintaining fixed exchange rates.

Is there any gain from devaluation under a fixed exchange rate system? One effect of devaluation is that the price level in the devaluing country may change relative to that in other countries. During and after this change, the rate of inflation and the nominal interest rate may be higher than they would otherwise have been. This means that the "tax" on money balances will be higher than it would otherwise have been, and more real resources will be used up economizing on money balances. This effect is likely to be rather small.

The other effect of devaluation is that it takes the pressure off of the exchange rate, and thus reduces the cost of intervention. It may reverse the direction of intervention, if it is large enough. If Britain was buying pounds with dollars and then devalues, it may find itself buying dollars with pounds, and thus reversing the direction of the change in its stock of reserves.

In a general equilibrium model, however, the principal effect of devaluation should be a fairly rapid adjustment of the relative price levels in various countries. The exact size of the change will depend on real factors and possibly on the countries' national monetary policies. Devaluation should have no appreciable impact on the balance of trade in the devaluing country. It should neither increase exports nor reduce imports significantly.[17]

Note also that devaluation does not normally hurt a country holding the devaluing country's bonds. There may be a loss on the date of the devaluation, but this will be offset by the fact that when devaluation is possible or likely, the bonds will tend to have higher interest rates than they would otherwise have. If individuals behave rationally, and choose to hold the bonds of two different countries in their portfolios, the interest rates must differ by an amount related to the difference in the probability rates of devaluation of the two currencies, other things being equal. Thus the premium interest rate received on the bonds of a country with a weak currency will tend to compensate the holder for the possible devaluation of that currency.

Taxation and Intervention Combined

Suppose that intervention is the basic policy being used to control exchange rates. Then it is possible that tax and other government policies will be used to take the pressure off of the exchange rate and reduce the amount of intervention required. The government may use tariffs, quotas, taxes on foreign investment, exchange controls, and other measures that we are describing broadly as "taxation."

While it is clear that taxation can be used to take the pressure off of the exchange rate, and thus to reduce or reverse the flow of foreign exchange reserves, it is not clear what kind of taxation should be used to reduce pressure in a particular direction. A country experiencing strong inflationary pressure may impose import taxes, export subsidies or both. These moves are likely to ease the pressure on the exchange rate, without reducing inflationary pressures within the country. Suppose, for example, that the "average price of goods" in the US is 10 dollars but is about to move up to 12 dollars. Suppose that the average price of the same goods in the UK is 4 pounds and is steady. Suppose that trade is balanced between the US and the UK, and that the equilibrium exchange rate in the absence of intervention is $2.50 to 1 pound.

When the US price level goes up, if nothing is done, the equilibrium exchange rate will go to $3.00 to 1 pound. But if a 20 percent tax is imposed on all imports, and a 20 percent export subsidy on all exports, the US price level can go up and the equilibrium exchange rate will still be $2.50 to 1 pound.

In other words, when a country increases its import taxes and its export subsidies, it will tend to cause its currency to depreciate at a rate less than its rate of inflation relative to other countries. This happens even though, under conditions of full employment, an import tax will not normally reduce imports substantially, and an export subsidy will not normally increase exports substantially.

Import taxes and export subsidies will change the pattern of consumption in two countries, especially when trade is not balanced and net foreign holdings of capital are not zero. But it is not clear whether the new pattern will result in an increase or a decrease in the country's trade balance. That will depend on the particulars of the situation.

Because of the way a country's balance of payments is usually described, it seems that the flow of foreign exchange reserves is a residual, and that the way to influence the residual is to influence the terms that are added and subtracted in calculating the residual. This is simply not correct. The government is not a principal in most current or capital account transactions, but it is a principal in foreign exchange transactions. Import taxes may have no effect on imports in a general equilibrium model; they may simply allow prices to rise while the equilibrium exchange rate stays relatively fixed.

The effects of taxes and subsidies on foreign holdings of domestic assets and on domestic holdings of foreign assets are more difficult to estimate. It seems, however, that a tax on domestic holdings of foreign assets will have the same effect as a tax on imports: it will take pressure off of the exchange rate in a country experiencing strong inflationary pressures relative to other countries. A subsidy on foreign holdings of domestic assets, or a combination of the tax and the subsidy, will work in the same direction.

Suppose, for example, that a country facing a 20 percent increase in its price level institutes a 20 percent tax on imports, a 20 percent subsidy on exports, a 20 percent tax on purchases of foreign securities or capital, and a 20 percent subsidy on sales of securities or capital to foreigners. If collected, these taxes and subsidies will balance out, to result in no net taxation. But they will just offset the 20 percent price rise, even in a country with a net flow or stock of foreign investment, so that the price rise can take place without a change in the equilibrium exchange rate.[18]

This combination of an increase in the price level and the institution of taxes and subsidies will have no real effects other than on the equilibrium exchange rate, so it is clear that just as tariffs should not be expected to affect imports, taxes on foreign investment should not be expected to affect capital flows. They will, however, serve to relieve pressure on the exchange rate, and thus to reduce the volume of intervention required to maintain a fixed exchange rate.

Intervention with Zero Reserves

It is often claimed that when inflationary pressures continue to be stronger in one country than in another, the government controlling the exchange rate cannot continue its intervention indefinitely, because its supply of reserves of foreign exchange would get too large, or because other countries' holdings of its liabilities would get too large. Even at the simplest level, this argument makes little sense in a world of general equilibrium and rational behavior.

If the government is holding larger and larger amounts of foreign exchange, then it will presumably be holding it in interest-bearing form. Assuming that interest is paid at a competitive rate, it will be compensated for holding the foreign exchange. If the government thinks that short-term bonds have low interest rates because they serve as a substitute for money, it can hold long-term bonds, or even equities.

The government can avoid increasing its money supply through its foreign exchange dealings by selling enough domestic bonds to offset its acquisition of foreign bonds. There will be no important limit to the amount of such domestic bonds it can sell, if it uses the foreign bonds as collateral in a way that guarantees the buyer of its domestic bonds that it cannot default on payment of principal or interest. Or it can run a budget surplus and raise the money it needs to buy the foreign bonds through taxation.

Similarly, if the government is having to borrow more and more foreign exchange to continue its intervention, it can do so in a way that minimizes the risk to the lenders. It can buy domestic bonds with the currency it receives (thus keeping the domestic money supply constant) and can use these bonds as collateral for its foreign exchange loans. With the collateral in the hands of the lenders, there should be no important limit to the amount of foreign exchange it can borrow.

In either case, the government will build up matching assets and liabilities denominated in the two different currencies. So it seems natural to ask whether the government can't simply give up its assets in payment of its liabilities, and thus keep its reserves near zero all the time.

In other words, the UK might do the following. It buys dollars with pounds in the ratio it is trying to maintain. It uses the dollars to buy long-term US government bonds. Then it sells the US government bonds for pounds to the highest bidder. In the process, it loses on transaction costs, and ends up with slightly fewer pounds than it started with.

Thus the UK could fix the exchange rate between pounds and dollars without running its foreign exchange balances up or down, and without changing its money supply. It could, in effect, fix exchange rates through intervention with zero reserves.

The result of using this method would be that the ratio of the price of US government bonds in dollars to the price in pounds would be slightly greater than the exchange rate being maintained. Any seller of bonds who wants pounds will sell for dollars and then convert them to pounds through the government, while any buyer of bonds with pounds will buy direct from the government. The gains to buyers and sellers of bonds for pounds will be losses to the government. Since the gains will be less than transaction costs in bonds, there will be no opportunity for continuous arbitrage against the government. The buyers and sellers will simply reduce their effective transaction costs.

It is clear that a government could adopt this policy; but it is not so clear that this policy would be effective in controlling exchange rates. It has been claimed that a country that dumps its foreign government bonds on the market in exchange for its own currency will be reversing its original support of the foreign currency.

It seems to me, however, that there are enough variables in the system for the policy to be effective. We have the foreign exchange rate, the price of US government bonds in dollars, and the price of US government bonds in pounds. By offering to buy unlimited quantities of dollars at the fixed rate, the UK ensures that the exchange rate (in pounds per dollar) cannot fall below that point. In buying US bonds for dollars and selling for pounds, it may drive the dollar price up slightly and the pound price down slightly, but it can't reduce the currency exchange rate.

Thus it seems that a country can fix its exchange rate with another country without allowing its support operations to affect either its money supply or its foreign exchange holdings. Since a fixed exchange rate, in the absence of changes in taxation, implies that the price level ratio changes only slowly through time, this means that a country should be able to control its price level and its money stock independently, even in the long run. That doesn't make sense, in a world of rational behavior, where the demand for money must always equal the supply. So something has to be wrong with the argument. I think that what is wrong is the assumption that a country can control its money supply in the first place. The contradiction derived above is yet another reason why it doesn't make sense to say that a government has any independent influence on a country's money supply.[19]

If we assume that each country's monetary policy is passive, so that it makes no attempt to control the money supply or interest rates, and that monetary factors do not enter into the determination of the price level, then the above conclusion can be made intelligible. It says simply that a country can control its exchange rate indefinitely without interfering with the natural growth or contraction of its money stock or of any other country's money stock. Demand factors and the factors that determine the price level (including exchange rate policy) will determine the money stock in each country.

Summary and Conclusions

Our assumption that individuals and firms behave rationally in the light of available information has led to the following conclusions:

1 Relative prices and quantities of all goods and services in an international monetary economy depend primarily on non-monetary factors. The only monetary effects arise from the influence of rates of inflation on the cost of economizing on money balances.

2 The factors that determine a country's trade balance and capital flows are entirely different from the factors that determine its balance of payments or volume of intervention. The country's trade balance and investment flows are determined primarily by the rate at which its residents want to spend or save out of their income and wealth. Its balance of payments or the volume of intervention needed to support the exchange rate is determined primarily by the strength of inflationary pressures in different countries.

3 The exchange rate between two countries can be allowed to float, or can be controlled through a combination of intervention and changes in tax policy. Floating exchange rates increase the cost of determining the prices of foreign goods, but this cost is likely to be minimal. Intervention can be very costly when differences in inflationary pressures are high. Changes in tax policy can worsen the distortions in international trade, and can thus reduce potential world welfare substantially. Thus floating exchange rates will almost always be best.

4 Devaluation or changes in taxes on trade and foreign investment can reduce the pressure on a fixed exchange rate, but will not have any obvious impact on the aggregate volume of imports, exports, or net foreign investment. The natural measure of a country's balance of payments is the direction and magnitude of intervention involving its currency.

5 Control of exchange rates through intervention does not require changes in a country's money supply or in its stock of foreign

exchange. It can be handled by acquiring bonds for one currency and disposing of the same bonds for the other currency. The losses in this operation can be made up by taxation.

6 Control of the exchange rate between two countries means control of the ratio of their price levels. If a closed economy could control its money stock then an open economy could, too. But independent control of two money stocks is inconsistent with control of the ratio of two price levels. Thus we have another piece of evidence that a government cannot control its country's money stock, but must adopt a passive monetary policy.

I am grateful to Stanley Black and Merton Miller for helpful comments on earlier versions of this chapter.

Notes

1 Cagan (1956) was one of the first writers to use adaptive expectations in an economic model. To use adaptive expectations on a time series, you form an expectation of the next observation in the series, and then revise the expectation by taking a weighted average of the expectation and the next observation, when the observation is available.
2 Muth (1961) has one of the early discussions of the implications of rational expectations. Gordon and Hynes (1970) show that Muth's analysis implies that adaptive expectations are generally not rational. Sargent (1971) has an analysis of the implications of rational expectations for the asserted trade-off between inflation and unemployment. Brock (1971) has looked at the implications of rational expectations for models of the behavior of firms in an industry.
3 Brock (1972) has explored the implications of rational expectations in a neoclassical monetary model. Chapter 2 of this book contains an analysis of the implications of rational economic behavior for monetary theory and monetary policy.
4 For an example of a "disequilibrium" theory that is not consistent with rational behavior, see Grossman (1971).
5 The precise conditions necessary for the existence of a unique competitive equilibrium are given, for example, by Quirk and Saposnik (1968).
6 The fact that it does not make sense to talk about devaluation in a "barter economy" has been pointed out by Dornbusch (1971). The present model is not really a model of a barter economy in the usual sense, since we assume the existence of securities, which can be used

to some degree in making trades. In a more general context, J. Black (1959) notes that with full employment, devaluation is not likely to have any real effects.

7 For discussion of these two approaches to devaluation, see Alexander (1952, 1959) and Machlup (1955). Their presentations do not assume full employment or the absence of money.

8 The distinction between flows of securities and flows of physical capital is often neglected, but has been made by others. For example, see Holmes (1972).

9 For an example of the many analyses that assume that capital flows are a response to interest rate differentials, see Sohmen (1967).

10 This point has been made, for example, by Borcich (1972).

11 There is no single obvious way to define the price level or rate of inflation in a country where a variety of goods and services are produced and consumed. We will assume that each country defines an arbitrary system for weighting the prices of various goods to determine a price level. The choice of a system for computing the price index will also determine the rate of inflation. If we define the real return on a security as the nominal return minus the rate of inflation, then real returns will also be arbitrary, in the sense that the real return that we calculate for any security will depend on the weighting used to determine the price level. Only in a one-commodity world is the real return on a security a more meaningful number than the nominal return.

12 For a discussion of some of the issues involved, see chapter 2.

13 Various monetary economists have presented models of the process, but the existing models are almost all inconsistent with rational behavior. For example, Friedman (1970) gives a model using adaptive expectations. And other economists give models in which the expected rate of inflation is taken to be equal to the rate of growth of the money supply, even during periods when the actual rate of inflation has differed from the rate of growth of the money supply.

14 For a summary of the "monetary approach" to balance of payments theory, see Johnson (1972).

15 See, for example, Mundell (1968, pp. 250–71).

16 The world's "potential welfare" is reduced if there is no set of transfers between individuals that would leave everyone at least as well off as before.

17 Laffer (1972) presents evidence that devaluation has in fact had little or no impact on the balance of trade of the devaluing country.

18 Others have noted that a uniform tax on imports and subsidy on exports which are also applied to capital transactions will have the same effect as a devaluation. For example, see the discussion between Aliber (1969) and Haberler (1969).

19 For the arguments in the context of a closed economy, see chapter 2.

References

Alexander, Sidney S. 1952: Effects of a devaluation on the trade balance. *International Monetary Fund Staff Papers*, 2, 263–78.

Alexander, Sidney S. 1959: Effects of a devaluation: a simplified synthesis of elasticities and absorption approaches. *American Economic Review*, 49, 22–42.

Aliber, Robert A. 1969: Improving the Bretton Woods system. In Robert A. Mundell and Alexander K. Swoboda (eds), *Monetary Problems of the International Economy*. Chicago: University of Chicago Press, 121–33.

Black, J. 1959: A saving and investment approach to devaluation. *Economic Journal*, 69, 267–74.

Borcich, John 1972: Capital flows, devaluation, and the balance of payments. *Canadian Journal of Economics*, 5, 215–26.

Brock, William A. 1971: On models of expectations that arise from maximizing behavior of economic agents over time. *Journal of Economic Theory*, 5, 348–76.

Brock, William A. 1972: Money and growth: the case of long run perfect foresight. Unpublished memorandum.

Cagan, Philip 1956: The monetary dynamics of hyperinflation. In Milton Friedman (ed.), *Studies in the Quantity Theory of Money*. Chicago: University of Chicago Press, 23–117.

Dornbusch, Rudiger 1971: Devaluation, relative prices and the real value of money. Center for Mathematical Studies in Business and Economics Report 7130, University of Chicago.

Friedman, Milton 1970: A theoretical framework for monetary analysis. *Journal of Political Economy*, 78, 193–238.

Gordon, Donald F. and Hynes, Allan 1970: On the theory of price dynamics. In Edmund S. Phelps (ed.), *Microeconomic Foundations of Employment and Inflation Theory*. New York: Norton, 369–93.

Grossman, Herschel I. 1971. Money, interest, and prices in market disequilibrium. *Journal of Political Economy*, 79, 943–61.

Haberler, Gottfried 1969: Taxes on imports and subsidies on exports as a tool of adjustment. In Robert A. Mundell and Alexander K. Swoboda (eds), *Monetary Problems of the International Economy*. Chicago: University of Chicago Press, 173–9.

Holmes, James M. 1972: The existence of capital flows, fixed and flexible exchange rates and full employment. *Canadian Journal of Economics*, 5, 215–26.

Johnson, Harry G. 1972: The monetary approach to balance of payments theory. *Journal of Financial and Quantitative Analysis*, 7, 1555–72.

Laffer, Arthur B. 1972. Exchange rates, the terms of trade, and the trade balance. Unpublished memorandum.

Machlup, Fritz 1955: Relative prices and aggregate spending in the analysis of devaluation. *American Economic Review*, 45, 255–78.

Mundell, Robert A. 1968: *International Economics*. New York: Macmillan.

Muth, John 1961: Rational expectations and the theory of price movements. *Econometrica*, 29, 315–35.

Quirk, James and Saposnik, Rubin 1968: *Introduction to General Equilibrium Theory and Welfare Economics*. New York: McGraw-Hill.

Sargent, Thomas J. 1971: A note on the accelerationist controversy. *Journal of Money, Credit, and Banking*, 3, 721–5.

Sohmen, Egon 1967: Fiscal and monetary policies under alternative exchange-rate systems. *Quarterly Journal of Economics*, 81, 515–23.

4

Uniqueness of the Price Level in Monetary Growth Models with Rational Expectations

Introduction

Almost every model of a monetary economy assumes that individuals and firms behave irrationally. They buy and sell goods at prices other than equilibrium prices, or they count the money the government gives them as wealth but ignore the fact that everyone else is getting money too, or they continue to expect zero inflation when the rate of inflation has been increasing for several periods. Monetary growth models[1] have moved in the direction of assuming rational behavior, but they have generally continued to assume that expectations about the rate of inflation are formed in an irrational manner. Following Cagan (1956), they typically assume some form of adaptive expectations, even when some other rule for revising expectations would give more accurate results.

In a model that does not include uncertainty in some explicit form, a straightforward way to put in rational expectations is to assume that individuals and firms have perfect foresight. One can then look at the set of paths for all economic variables such that each individual is maximizing his or her utility and each firm is maximizing its value, at every point in time, in the light of the current and future values of all the variables. Each such path is a "competitive equilibrium" consistent with rational economic behavior.[2]

In a world with well-developed financial markets, it is not easy to describe a mechanism by which changes in monetary policy or

Reprinted with permission from *Journal of Economic Theory*, Vol. 7, No. 1, January 1974. Copyright ©1974 by Academic Press, Inc.

changes in the money supply itself will lead to changes in the price level or rate of inflation.[3] The problem is similar to the one we encounter in general equilibrium models of exchange. There it is difficult to describe the mechanism by which a set of prices is determined at which everyone can exchange his endowment for a preferred collection of goods, and such that the total demand for each good equals the supply. The solution adopted in that case is simply to ignore the mechanism by which equilibrium is achieved, and to investigate the existence and uniqueness of a set of prices and an allocation of goods that equates total demand and total supply of each good, and that gives each individual goods worth the same as his initial endowment. Under certain conditions there will be only one such competitive equilibrium, and it is plausible to assume that the economy would reach that equilibrium, even though we cannot specify the exact process by which it is reached.

Those who believe that the money supply can be and is determined by the central bank in a modern economy might like to use this same technique. Since it is difficult to describe a mechanism by which a given monetary policy will cause an economy of rational individuals to follow a certain path, they might like to sidestep the description of such a mechanism, and ask about the existence of a unique path for the economy consistent with the given monetary policy. Finding that there is only one competitive equilibrium path consistent with a given monetary policy will not prove that the given policy will cause the economy to follow that path, but such a finding would allow us to concentrate our attention on that path and its properties. Finding that there are many paths consistent with a given monetary policy will make this technique useless. We will have to go back to the search for a mechanism for the transmission of monetary policy to determine which, if any, of these paths will be followed.

Brock (1972) has taken this approach in a model of an economy in which everyone lives for the same period (which may be infinite), and in which money is the only store of wealth. He finds that, if the money stock is assumed to be constant through time, there is only one path for the price level and other variables along which the conditions for equilibrium are always satisfied. (It is a path along which the price level is constant.) On the other hand, he finds that an attempt to satiate the economy with real balances by decreasing nominal balances at a certain rate will often be consistent with a whole range of paths for the price level and other variables. Thus in one case he finds a unique perfect foresight path consistent with a given monetary policy, and in another case he does not.

I believe that perfect foresight is the only assumption consistent with rational behavior in a model without uncertainty. It may be that, if the monetary authorities control the money stock, the best model for their behavior is one in which only random changes in the money stock occur. If this is true, then it is likely that the economy would operate more smoothly if the authorities changed to a policy of zero or constant growth in the money stock. However, it is interesting to ask what would happen if there were non-random elements in monetary policy. For example, it would be interesting to know the consequences of a policy that involves changing the rate of growth of the money supply in response to such economic variables as the rate of inflation and the level of perceived unemployment. In this chapter, we will be concerned primarily with monetary policies that are responsive to changes in the past rate of inflation. For this purpose, the explicit inclusion of uncertainty in the model will only complicate the analysis.

It has already been noted that, if individuals form expectations about the rate of inflation rationally, and if inflation has a negative effect on the demand for money, then there may be many paths for the price level consistent with a constant rate of growth in the money stock.[4] For each initial price level, there is a different path. Most of these paths involve a constantly increasing or decreasing rate of inflation.

Sargent and Wallace deal with these issues in a model assuming perfect foresight (1973b) and in a model including an explicit form of uncertainty (1973a). They imagine that a new monetary policy has just been announced, and that, after the economy adjusts to the announcement, no further changes in policy will take place. They assume that the price level can jump following the announcement of a new monetary policy. In the case of perfect foresight, there can be no further jumps in the price level, since a jump that is foreseen will imply a zero (if the jump is up) or infinite (if the jump is down) demand for money at the time of the jump. Their models are at a more aggregated level than those of Brock (1972): while their models are consistent with maximizing behavior on the part of individuals, they do not write down individual utility functions explicitly. They write the aggregate demand for money as a function of the price level and the current rate of inflation. They note that there may be many paths consistent with a policy of constant growth in the money supply, but that all but one of these involve a continually increasing or decreasing rate of inflation. They rule out such paths as being "unreasonable." Thus, for each monetary policy that they consider, there is a unique subsequent path for the price level such that equilibrium conditions are always satisfied and such that the rate of inflation is bounded.

In this chapter, we will also use an aggregate demand for money function, and will assume that the demand for money depends on present and possibly future values for the price level and rate of inflation. A more complete model might assume that the demand for money depends on present and possibly future values of the nominal interest rate rather than the rate of inflation. However, instead of assuming that the entire path for the money stock is specified at the time a new monetary policy is announced, we will generally assume that the rate of growth of the money stock is made a function of the rate of inflation in the period just past.

In particular, we will assume that the rate of growth of the money supply is a multiple greater than one of the past rate of inflation. An increase in the rate of inflation is met with an even larger increase in the rate of growth of the money stock, and a decrease in the rate of inflation is met with a larger decrease in the rate of growth of the money stock.[5] We do not mean to imply that this is a policy that is used or should be used by the central bank. But, if you believe that the central bank can control the money stock, this is one type of policy that it might choose. If the equilibrium path for the price level consistent with a monetary policy of this kind is not unique, then the approach of selecting the unique economic path consistent with a given monetary policy seems unsatisfactory. We will be forced back to investigations of the mechanism by which monetary policy might affect the economy.

The Basic Model

We will assume that changes in the money stock and the price level are independent of changes in real factors such as the level of employment and the rate of consumption.[6] We will assume that the population is stable. We will write P_t for the price level at time t, and M_t for the aggregate nominal money stock at time t. In this first model, we will assume that the money stock is constant, so we will write it simply as M.

Following Sargent and Wallace (1973b), we will write the demand for real balances as a simple function of the next period's rate of inflation:

$$\log(M/P_t) = -\beta\log(P_{t+1}/P_t). \tag{4.1}$$

In equation (4.1), β is positive. Replacing t by $t-1$ in equation (4.1), we get equation (4.2):

$$\log(M/P_{t-1}) = -\beta\log(P_t/P_{t-1}). \tag{4.2}$$

Subtracting equation (4.2) from equation (4.1), we get:

$$\log(P_t/P_{t-1}) = \beta[\log(P_{t+1}/P_t) - \log(P_t/P_{t-1})]. \tag{4.3}$$

Now let us define y_t as the log of the ratio of two price levels. It is similar to a rate of inflation.

$$y_t = \log(P_{t+1}/P_t). \tag{4.4}$$

Substituting from definition (4.4) in equation (4.3), we have:

$$y_{t-1} = \beta(y_t - y_{t-1}). \tag{4.5}$$

Collecting the terms involving y_{t-1}, and dividing through by β, this becomes:

$$y_t = (1 + 1/\beta)y_{t-1}. \tag{4.6}$$

The solution to equation (4.6) may be written:

$$y_t = (1 + 1/\beta)^t y_0. \tag{4.7}$$

In other words, if the initial value of y_0 is positive, the rate of inflation increases exponentially. If the initial value of y_0 is negative, the rate of deflation increases exponentially over time. Setting $t = 0$ in equation (4.1), we may write:

$$y_0 = -\log(M/P_0)/\beta. \tag{4.8}$$

Thus, for every initial value of P_0, equation (4.8) gives an initial value of y_0, and equation (4.7) gives the complete path of the rate of inflation. There is a price level path consistent with every possible choice of the initial price level.

Intuitively, what is happening is that the higher the initial price level, the lower is the initial level of real balances, thus the higher the initial rate of inflation must be for the demand for real balances to equal the supply. But a high rate of inflation means that the supply of real balances will be decreasing over time, which means that the rate of inflation must continue to increase if demand is always to equal the supply. This gives an accelerating rate of inflation. If the initial price level is low, then the initial rate of inflation will be negative, and we will have an accelerating rate of deflation.

Only if the initial price level is consistent with a zero rate of inflation will the price level be constant through time. If we say that the demand for money function described by equation (4.1) breaks down for very large rates of inflation or deflation, then we can rule out all paths but this one as being inconsistent with rational behavior and perfect foresight.

Adaptive Monetary Policy

Now let us assume that, instead of specifying a constant money stock, we increase the money stock over the next period at a rate that depends on last period's rate of inflation:

$$\log(M_{t+1}/M_t) = k\log(P_t/P_{t-1}), \quad k > 1. \tag{4.9}$$

Assuming that $k > 1$ means assuming that an increase or decrease in the rate of inflation is followed by a greater increase or decrease in the rate of growth of the money stock. Let us define x_t as a measure of the rate of growth of the money stock as follows:

$$x_t = \log(M_{t+1}/M_t). \tag{4.10}$$

Let us rewrite equation (4.1), putting a time subscript on the money stock:

$$\log(M_t/P_t), = -\beta\log(P_{t+1}/P_t), \quad \beta > 1. \tag{4.11}$$

By assuming $\beta > 1$, we are assuming that the demand for money is "sufficiently sensitive" to the rate of inflation. Putting $t+1$ for t in equation (4.11), we have:

$$\log(M_{t+1}/P_{t+1}) = -\beta\log(P_{t+2}/P_{t+1}). \tag{4.12}$$

Subtracting equation (4.12) from equation (4.11), we get:

$$\log(M_{t+1}/M_t) - \log(P_{t+1}/P_t) \\ = -\beta[\log(P_{t+2}/P_{t+1}) - \log(P_{t+1}/P_t)]. \tag{4.13}$$

Substituting from definitions (4.4) and (4.10) in equation (4.13), we get:

$$x_t - y_t = -\beta(y_{t+1} - y_t).\qquad(4.14)$$

Substituting in equation (4.9), we get:

$$x_t = ky_{t-1}.\qquad(4.15)$$

Substituting from equation (4.15) in equation (4.14), we have:

$$ky_{t-1} - y_t = -\beta(y_{t+1} - y_t).\qquad(4.16)$$

Equation (4.16) may be rewritten as follows:

$$\beta y_{t+1} - (1+\beta)y_t + ky_{t-1} = 0.\qquad(4.17)$$

Equation (4.17) is a second-order, linear, difference equation. The standard method for solving such an equation is to look for two solutions of the form $y_t = \lambda^t$. The general solution will be a linear combination of these two specific solutions. Substituting that expression for y_t into equation (4.17), and dividing through by λ^{t-1}, we have:

$$\beta\lambda^2 - (1+\beta)\lambda + k = 0.\qquad(4.18)$$

The solutions to the quadratic equation (4.18) are given by:

$$\lambda = (1/2\beta)[(1+\beta) \pm \sqrt{1 + 2\beta + \beta^2 - 4k\beta}].\qquad(4.19)$$

When $k=1$, the two solutions are $1/\beta$ and 1. When $k>1$, both solutions are either between zero and one or complex. If they are complex, their real parts are both between zero and one.

Thus, when $\beta>1$ and $k>1$, λ_1^t and λ_2^t both converge to zero. The general solution to equation (4.17) may be written as follows:

$$y_t = a_1\lambda_1^t + a_2\lambda_2^t.\qquad(4.20)$$

This means that y_t also converges to zero as t gets large. No matter what its initial value, the rate of inflation goes to zero along a price level path consistent with the given monetary policy.

To complete our specification of the monetary policy, we must give values for M_0 and M_1. We can choose an initial price level, P_0, arbitrarily. Then equations (4.10) and (4.11) give the initial values x_0 and y_0. Putting $t=0$ in equation (4.20), we get:

$$a_1 + a_2 = y_0.\qquad(4.21)$$

Putting $t=0$ in equation (4.14), rearranging, and substituting from equation (4.20) with $t=1$, we get:

$$\beta(a_1\lambda_1 + a_2\lambda_2) - (1+\beta)y_0 + x_0 = 0. \tag{4.22}$$

Given the values of x_0, y_0, β, λ_1, and λ_2, equations (4.21) and (4.22) allow us to solve for a_1 and a_2.

Thus, for the given monetary policy, including a choice of M_0 and M_1, each choice of an initial price level gives us a different price level path consistent with perfect foresight and with continual equilibrium in the money market. Furthermore, each of these paths converges to a zero rate of inflation, so none can be ruled out on the grounds that the rate of inflation is unbounded.

With an adaptive monetary policy of this kind, neither the initial price level nor the future path of the price level is determined uniquely by the assumption of rational behavior. And all of the possible paths, except those with very large or very small values of P_0, are reasonable.

Future Rates of Inflation and Money Demand

So far, we have assumed that the demand for money depends only on the current price level and next period's rate of inflation. It is reasonable to suppose, however, that the demand for money might depend on the anticipated rates of inflation for other periods as well. Most generally, it might depend on all future rates of inflation.

To illustrate the properties of such a model, let us assume a money demand function of the following form:

$$\log(M_t/P_t) = -\beta \sum_{s=0}^{\infty} \gamma^s \log(P_{t+s+1}/P_{t+s}), \quad \beta > 1, \ \gamma < 1. \tag{4.23}$$

This means that more distant future rates of inflation affect the demand for money less than nearer rates of inflation. We will continue to assume that monetary policy is given by equation (4.9) or (4.15), together with values for M_0 and M_1. Putting $t+1$ for t in equation (4.23), and changing the range of s, we have:

$$\log(M_{t+1}/P_{t+1}) = -\beta \sum_{s=1}^{\infty} \gamma^{s-1} \log(P_{t+s+1}/P_{t+s}). \tag{4.24}$$

Substituting from definition (4.4), and pulling $(1/\gamma)$ out of the summation, we have:

$$\log(M_{t+1}/P_{t+1}) = -(\beta/\gamma) \sum_{s=1}^{\infty} \gamma^s y_{t+s}. \tag{4.25}$$

The summation can be rewritten, to give:

$$\log(M_{t+1}/P_{t+1}) = -(\beta/\gamma)\left[\sum_{s=0}^{\infty} \gamma^s y_{t+s} - y_t\right]. \qquad (4.26)$$

But the first term on the right-hand side of (4.26) can be rewritten, using equation (4.23), to give:

$$\log(M_{t+1}/P_{t+1}) = (1/\gamma)\log(M_t/P_t) + (\beta/\gamma)y_t. \qquad (4.27)$$

Putting $t - 1$ for t in equation (4.27), and subtracting the resulting equation from equation (4.27), we get:

$$x_t - y_t = (1/\gamma)(x_{t-1} - y_{t-1}) + (\beta/\gamma)(y_t - y_{t-1}). \qquad (4.28)$$

Multiplying through by γ, and rearranging, we get:

$$\gamma x_t - x_{t-1} - (\gamma+\beta)y_t + (1+\beta)y_{t-1} = 0. \qquad (4.29)$$

Substituting from equation (4.15), we get:

$$\gamma k y_{t-1} - k y_{t-2} - (\gamma+\beta)y_t + (1+\beta)y_{t-1} = 0. \qquad (4.30)$$

Equation (4.30) rearranges to:

$$(\gamma+\beta)y_t - (1+\beta+\gamma k)y_{t-1} + k y_{t-2} = 0. \qquad (4.31)$$

Again we have a second-order, linear, difference equation. If it has two basic solutions that both converge, then we know that we will again have a whole family of reasonable price paths consistent with the given monetary policy. To find the basic solutions, we put $y_t = \lambda^t$, and divide through by λ^{t-2}:

$$(\gamma+\beta)\lambda^2 - (1+\beta+\gamma k)\lambda + k = 0. \qquad (4.32)$$

The solutions to equation (4.32) are given by:

$$\lambda = [1+\beta+\gamma k \pm \sqrt{(1+\beta+\gamma k)^2 - 4k(\gamma+\beta)}]/2(\gamma+\beta). \qquad (4.33)$$

Writing α for $\gamma+\beta$, and setting $k=1$, this becomes:

$$\lambda = [1+\alpha \pm \sqrt{(1-\alpha)^2}]/2\alpha \qquad (4.34)$$

The two values of λ under these circumstances are 1 and $1/\alpha$. By taking the derivative of equation (4.33) with respect to k, it can be shown that increasing k causes both roots to be less than one. But, for very large values of k and any positive value of γ, one root will be greater than one. So it is values of k moderately larger than one that will give two values for λ, both between zero and one.

For a monetary policy with a value of k in this range, there will again be a reasonable price level path for every value of P_0 that is not too large or too small. Even though the demand for money depends on future as well as current rates of inflation, the price level path consistent with a given monetary policy of the type we are considering will not be unique.

Uncertainty

The lack of uniqueness that we have found for perfect foresight paths seems likely to carry over to the case of a model including uncertainty, since certainty is the limiting case of uncertainty as the degree of uncertainty goes to zero. To verify this, let us look at a simple model involving uncertainty.

We will assume that the price level path follows a stochastic process described by the following equation:

$$\log(\tilde{P}_{t+1}/P_t) = N(\mu_t, \sigma_t^2). \tag{4.35}$$

In other words, $\tilde{P}_{t+1}/P_t$ is distributed lognormally with parameters μ_t and σ_t^2.

We will assume that the demand for money depends on both of the parameters of this distribution, as follows:

$$\log(M_t/P_t) = -\beta\mu_t - \gamma\sigma_t^2, \quad \beta > 0, \ \gamma > 0. \tag{4.36}$$

We will continue to assume that monetary policy is described by equation (4.9) plus the values of M_0 and M_1.

The stochastic process generating the path of prices will be specified if we give a rule for determining all of the values of μ_t and σ_t^2. There are a variety of ways in which this could be done. For example, we might choose arbitrary values for $\sigma_0^2, \sigma_1^2, \sigma_2^2, \ldots$ going on forever. We can choose an arbitrary value for P_0, and equation (4.36) will give an initial value for μ_0. After P_1 is determined by a "drawing," equation (4.36) will give μ_1. A new drawing gives P_2, and equation (4.9) gives M_2. This determines the stochastic path of P_t.

We might also take the values of $\mu_0, \mu_1, \mu_2, \ldots$ going on forever to be arbitrary, and use equation (4.36) to determine the values of σ_t^2. Again we can choose P_0 arbitrarily, along with all of the values of μ_t. It is clear that we are working with a family of paths that has an infinite number of parameters that can be chosen arbitrarily. The lack of uniqueness of the process generating the price level path is even worse if we introduce uncertainty.

Note that we have assumed in this analysis that the parameters of the process generating the price level are always known to individuals. Thus they are assumed to form their expectations about the future of the price level in a rational manner.

Adaptive Expectations

Those who construct models that do not assume rational economic behavior often use a device called "adaptive expectations." In a discrete model, this means assuming that next period's expected rate of inflation $\log(P_{t+1}/P_t)^e$ is determined by an equation of the following type:

$$\log(P_{t+1}/P_t)^e - \log(P_t/P_{t-1})^e$$
$$= \gamma[\log(P_t/P_{t-1}) - \log(P_t/P_{t-1})^e], \quad \gamma < 1. \qquad (4.37)$$

In other words, it is assumed that the expected rate of inflation is revised by an amount proportional to the error in last period's expected rate of inflation.

This method of revising expectations is almost always irrational.[7] It means that, if the rate of inflation goes to a new level and stays there, the expected rate of inflation will approach that level only gradually. The expected rate of inflation will be consistently higher or lower than the actual rate of inflation.

In a model using this device, the demand for real balances is usually written as a function of the expected rate of inflation, such as the following:

$$\log(M_t/P_t) = -\beta\log(P_{t+1}/P_t)^e. \qquad (4.38)$$

Now what happens when a change in monetary policy is announced? These models usually assume that the expected rate of inflation continues to be revised according to equation (4.37), and that information about the new monetary policy does not influence the expected rate of inflation at all. This is clearly not a reasonable way to revise one's expectations.

But, even if we assume that the announcement causes no change in the expected rate of inflation, we do not have enough information to determine the price path in the future. The announcement will in general cause the actual price level to start out at a new level. The comparison of this new level with the level that was expected under the old monetary policy is not a reasonable thing to use in revising our expectations, so we cannot use equation (4.37) to make the first revision in our expected rate of inflation. We have no rational basis for choosing the first revision. For each choice we make, we get a different price path for the future.

Again, there are many paths for the price level consistent with a newly announced monetary policy.

Conclusions

Our results can be stated intuitively as follows. When a new monetary policy is announced, there are many combinations of a new price level and rate of inflation that will make individuals happy to hold the existing stock of real balances. Suppose, for example, that the new monetary policy includes an immediate doubling of the nominal stock of money. There are many jumps in the price level that would be consistent with this. The price level may double, with no change in the rate of inflation. Or the price level may more than double, causing a decline in real balances, and the rate of inflation may increase, causing an appropriate reduction in the demand for real balances. Finally, the price level may less than double, and the rate of inflation may decrease, causing an increase in real balances and an equal increase in the demand for real balances.

If we must choose among these possibilities, the second seems the most plausible. An upward jump in the price level means that the rate of inflation becomes very large. To say that the rate of inflation gets very large and then goes back to exactly the level it had before the jump seems very odd. It seems more likely that it might settle back to a level higher than the original level.

The important conclusion, however, is that the assumption of rational behavior alone does not allow us to choose one from among the many possible paths. We do not have a single competitive equilibrium, as we often do in a non-monetary growth model.[8] We have many competitive equilibria. Thus we cannot ignore the mechanism by which monetary policy supposedly influences the price level and other economic variables. We need a detailed microeconomic model of a monetary economy to have any hope of being able to decide which, if any, of these paths the economy follows.

The monetary policies discussed in this chapter are all comparable to the "active" monetary policies discussed in chapter 2. Thus the lack of uniqueness discussed here is not the same as the indeterminacy of the price level in some models that assume "passive" monetary policy. The basic monetary policy examined in this chapter, where next period's growth in the money stock depends on last period's inflation, could be said to imply an "endogenous" money supply, but it assumes that the central bank can fix the money supply in response to whatever economic variables it wants to use. Passive monetary policy, on the other hand, means that the central bank has no influence on the money stock; and that changes in the money stock are caused entirely by changes in the demand for money.

I am grateful to William Brock, Stanley Fischer, Milton Friedman, Arthur Laffer, Merton Miller, David Ranson, Thomas Sargent, Charles Upton, and a referee for ideas and comments on earlier drafts of this chapter.

Notes

1 For example, see Sidrauski (1967).
2 This approach has been developed most completely by Brock (1972).
3 For a detailed discussion of these issues, see chapter 2.
4 See chapter 2; also Sidrauski (1967), Burmeister and Dobell (1970, chapter 6), and Olivera (1979, 1971).
5 This type of monetary policy has been investigated by Goldman (1972) in the context of a model assuming adaptive expectations.
6 Lucas (1972) tries to look at the interaction between the price level, the rate of inflation, and the level of unemployment in a model that assumes rational behavior in the presence of uncertainty. His model would have multiple solutions for the price level and rate of inflation, but he assumes away this possibility by stating that the price level must depend only on real factors plus the money stock, and cannot depend on past rates of inflation.
7 Muth (1961) has shown that adaptive expectations can be rational in a discrete time model if there is just the right amount of first-order negative serial correlation in the series being forecast, and no higher order serial correlation.
8 For example, see Diamond (1965).

References

Brock, W. A. 1972: Money and growth: the case of long run perfect foresight. Unpublished memorandum.
Burmeister, E. and Dobell, A. R. 1970: *Mathematical Theories of Economic Growth*. New York: Macmillan.

Cagan, P. 1956: The monetary dynamics of hyperinflation. In M. Friedman (ed.), *Studies in the Quantity Theory of Money*, Chicago: University of Chicago Press, 25–120.

Diamond, P. 1965: National debt in a neoclassical growth model. *American Economic Review*, 55, 1126–50.

Goldman, S. M. 1972: Hyperinflation and the rate of growth in the money supply. *Journal of Economic Theory*, 5, 250–7.

Lucas, R. E. Jr. 1972: Expectations and the neutrality of money. *Journal of Economic Theory*, 4, 103–24.

Muth, J. 1961: Rational expectations and the theory of price movements. *Econometrica*, 29, 315–35.

Olivera, J. H. 1970: On passive money. *Journal of Political Economy*, 78, 805–14.

Olivera, J. H. 1971: A note on passive money, inflation, and economic growth. *Journal of Money, Credit, and Banking*, 3, 137–44.

Sargent, T. J. and Wallace, N. 1973a: Rational expectations and the dynamics of hyperinflation. *International Economic Review*, 14, 328–50.

Sargent, T. J. and Wallace, N. 1973b: The stability of models of money and growth with perfect foresight. *Econometrica*, 41, 1043–8.

Sidrauski, M. 1967: Inflation and economic growth. *Journal of Political Economy*, 75, 796–810.

5

Purchasing Power Parity in an Equilibrium Model

Let us assume a world where each country produces and consumes a different bundle of goods and services; where there are transport costs, taxes, and direct controls on the movement of currency, securities, goods, and people; and where countries intervene in exchange markets from time to time to influence exchange rates.

The "official" exchange rate between two countries is the rate at which one or both of the countries will exchange their currencies. If one government stands ready to exchange the two currencies with any individual or institution in unlimited amounts at the official exchange rate, then the "effective" exchange rate will be equal to the official exchange rate. If the government will exchange currencies at the official rate only with specific individuals or institutions under specific circumstances, then the effective rate or the "market" rate will often differ from the official rate. If the government bans transactions at other than the official rate, and places limits on individual and institutional holdings of foreign exchange, then the free market rate will be a "black market" rate. The most interesting economic variable is the market exchange rate for a pair of countries that do not restrict private transactions in their currencies. This can occur under fixed rates, flexible rates, or mixed systems such as pegged rates or flexible rates with intervention.

When private transactions are restricted, then the exchange rate will depend on who the transactors are. There will not be a single exchange rate at a given point in time. The black market rates will reflect the penalties the government will impose if a transaction is discovered and the likelihood that it will be discovered.

The law of one price says that when there are no transport costs, taxes, or direct controls, and when there is a market exchange rate at which everyone can exchange currencies freely, then the price of a good or service in one country times the exchange rate must equal

74

the price of the same good or service in the other country. Even services are covered by this law, because assuming no transport costs means that customers can be brought without cost to the country in which the service is provided.

The law of one price is self-evident to most of us, at least as a theoretical proposition. It is still interesting to "test" it, in the sense that we look at an apparent violation of the law, and try to find out what factors explain the apparent violation. We may be comparing goods that are not identical, or transport costs may be important, or import taxes or controls may be effective or exchange transactions may not be allowed to occur freely at the market rate.

The law of one equilibrium is just as self-evident as the law of one price to some of us. It says that for a given set of real conditions in the world, including transport costs, taxes, and direct controls, there will be a single set of equilibrium relative prices (and quantities) for all goods and services. Among the relative prices that are determined by real factors are the price of any traded good relative to the price of any non-traded good, the relative price of any pair of non-traded goods in the same country, and the price of any non-traded good in one country relative to the price of the same good in another country. There is no special reason for distinguishing between traded and non-traded goods. Monetary factors can at most affect the price levels, rates of inflation, and exchange rates between two countries. Monetary factors will not affect the relative price of any pair of goods.

Relative prices do change over time, because the real conditions in the world change over time. So we can't test the law of one equilibrium by testing whether relative prices are constant. We can test it, however, by looking at periods in which government policy changes radically. If a government changes the exchange rate between two countries, and if the exchange rates both before and after the change are market exchange rates at which currencies may be exchanged freely, and if there are no offsetting changes in taxes or direct controls at the same time, then we expect that the relative price of any pair of goods will be unchanged. To distinguish this test from a test of the law of one price, we might apply the test to a non-traded good in the two countries.

Another way to "test" the law of one equilibrium is to look at apparent violations of the law and try to explain them. If a pure devaluation (as defined above) seems to cause a change in some relative price, then we will look for some explanation. Perhaps the relative price was going to change anyway. Perhaps the devaluation was not so pure, and there were some significant changes in taxes or direct controls along with it. Perhaps there are errors in our price data. This a legitimate test in the sense that one can imagine finding that the data are truly inconsistent with the hypothesis. In another sense, the test is a waste of time, because it is so unlikely that the law of one equilibrium is false.

The purchasing power parity theorem is derived from the law of one equilibrium. It says that the relative price of a particular bundle of goods and services in one country and a particular bundle of goods and services in another country is determined entirely by real factors. This theorem, like the other two propositions discussed above, makes sense only when there is a market exchange rate between the two countries at which their currencies may be exchanged freely. The particular bundle of goods and services used in each country is the bundle used in calculating the price index in that country.

The purchasing power parity theorem is harder to test than either the law of one price or the law of one equilibrium, because it makes use of prices for such a large number of goods and services. There are likely to be substantial errors in some of these prices. And there are likely to be substantial changes over time in the relative prices of some pairs of items from the two indexes. The more the two indexes differ in composition, the more substantial are the changes we expect over time in the relative price of the two bundles.

The purchasing power parity theorem, as defined above, holds all the time. It holds in the short run and in the long run. To test it, we would look for changes in government exchange rate policy that occur for two countries with (a) a market exchange rate both before and after the change in policy, (b) no changes in taxes or direct controls along with the change in policy, (c) no sharp changes in relative prices for reasons unrelated to exchange rates, and (d) relatively error-free price indexes.

We can do another test by ignoring (a) – (d), and simply comparing changes in exchange rates and changes in price indexes. Since we are ignoring so many important factors, it would be surprising to find the data consistent with purchasing power parity, especially in the short run. In the long run, some of these factors should wash out. Thus it is very surprising that Moon Hoe Lee[1] finds the data so consistent with the theorem, both in the short run and in the long run. He finds a good relationship in the short run even without taking violation of (a) – (d) into account, and he finds an amazingly close relationship in the long run.

Notes

1 See Lee (1976).

References

Lee, Moon H. *Purchasing Power Parity*. New York: Marcel Dekker, 1976.

6

Ups and Downs in Human Capital and Business

We can think of a person's human capital as his ability to earn money. How much he will actually earn at various times in the future will depend on what happens and on what he decides to do; but his human capital sums up the value of the ways he has of turning effort into income. We can almost think of the value of a person's human capital as the present value of his uncertain future income, just as we think of the value of a stock as the present value of its uncertain future dividends. All this leaves out is the effect on the person of the work he has to do to get the income.

The value of a person's human capital certainly fluctuates over time. A baby's human capital, for example, changes after the doctor first examines him: if any serious defects are found, the value of the baby's human capital goes down; and if everything seems all right, the value of the baby's human capital goes up.

For a time, a child's human capital is closely tied to its parent's human capital. If a parent loses his job, the child's human capital goes down in value along with the parent's. Later, the child is on his own. He may work for a large company, though, and his human capital may go up and down in value along with the company's stock. When things look good for the company, things look good for him. When things look bad for the company, things look bad for him.

If just one company is affected, the person can look for a new job with another company. But if all the companies that use his skills are affected he will be affected too. An employee's chances to earn money are affected some by the fortunes of his company, some by the fortunes of all the companies in the same business, and some by the fortunes of all the companies there are.

If we add together everybody's human capital, we get the economy's human capital, or total human capital. Since each individual's human capital tends to go up and down with the prospects for the business he is in, total human capital tends to go up and down with the prospects for businesses generally. The best measure we have of the prospects for businesses generally is the stock market. So the value of total human capital tends to go up and down with the level of the stock market.

This isn't really very surprising. When the economy is booming, things are good for business and jobs are easy to find and keep. When the economy is lagging, profits are down, and overtime is cut, and people are laid off, and lots of people don't even bother to look for a job. When times are good for business, times are good for labor; and when times are bad for business, times are bad for labor.

It's true, of course, that labor sometimes gains at the expense of business, and that business sometimes gains at the expense of labor. But each side is limited by strong economic forces. If a labor union negotiates magnificent increases in wages and benefits, it may find that many of its members are unemployed, and that employers using non-union labor get more business than employers in the same industry using union labor. Some employers may even go out of business.

Generally, the factors that cause shifts between business and labor are dwarfed by the factors that cause them to go up and down together. The problems that business has at times cannot usually be blamed on the success of labor, and the problems that labor has cannot usually be blamed on the oppression of business. They both have problems at the same time. And their problems stem, as we shall see, from the same sources.

Capital and Labor

Even the simplest economic models suggest that human capital and physical capital wax and wane together. The simplest models have people working with machines to produce either more machines or other goods and services that are in demand. The machines are called "capital," the people are called "labor," and what they produce is called "output."

If a person has more machines to work with, or better machines, then he can produce more. If he can produce more, he can earn more. Thus the more capital there is, the more people earn. The more physical capital there is, the more the economy's human capital is worth.

This means that investments in physical capital increase the value of human capital. And it works the other way, too: if a person is better educated, or learns more job-related skills, he can often produce more with the same machine. So investments in human capital increase the value of physical capital.

In fact, some economists argue that for many purposes there is no reason to distinguish between different kinds of capital. We can not only lump together machines, tools, real estate, and inventories; we can also lump all these together with human capital.

Capital, thus summed up, fluctuates in value even if we don't put anything in or take anything out. Its value also changes over time in a way that depends on how fast we are spending on things other than new capital. Faster spending means slower growth in capital, and slower spending means faster growth in capital. Or, if the value of capital would be declining anyway, faster spending means a faster decline, and slower spending means a slower decline. The way to stimulate "capital formation," especially in the long run, is to cut down on both government and private spending.

And in fact, we do respond to changes in the value of capital by changing our spending habits. When the value of capital goes up, we tend to step up our spending, and when the value of capital goes down, we tend to cut back our spending. For a more detailed analysis of the relation between capital and spending, see the early chapters of Miller and Upton (1974).

Let's keep in mind, in thinking about total capital, that human capital is probably the bulk of it. Even if we add real estate and other personal property to the value of business capital, the value of human capital is probably well over half of the total. So if we have to think of capital as being either physical or human, we're better off thinking of it as human.

Human capital, though, is produced just as much as physical capital is produced. A raw human being has about as much economic value as an uncultivated piece of land in the wilderness. Through his own efforts and through the efforts of others, a person takes on education, socialization, and experience that increase his economic value just as surely as roads, sewers, utilities, and buildings increase the value of a piece of land.

The Sources of Uncertainty

Why do human capital and business have ups and downs that are largely unpredictable? I think it's because of basic uncertainty about what people will want in the future and about what the economy will be able to produce in the future. If future tastes and technology were known, profits and wages would grow smoothly and surely over time.

What happens is that people estimate what the future will be like, using all the available information. Then they decide how to invest in human or physical capital. They choose an occupation, or decide between formal education and on-the-job training, or move from a slow-growing area to a fast-growing area of the country. They choose between a highly automated plant and one that takes less of an initial outlay but uses more people. They choose between building more fast-food outlets on highways and setting up employee cafeterias in large office buildings.

To a significant extent, these decisions are irreversible. When it turns out that the decisions are right, the businesses that made them and the people who decided to work for those businesses do well. When it turns out that the decisions are wrong, everyone does badly. When high gas costs keep people away from fast-food outlets, both the restaurant owners and the employees end up wishing they had invested differently.

If all these decisions could somehow be made independently, perhaps the errors would cancel out, and the future course of the economy would be smooth. But they can't be made independently. They must be based on the information we have now. If that information is wrong, it will be wrong in the same direction for everyone. (Except that a few people may have ignored the information or may have assumed that it was wrong.)

Thus the source of the ups and downs in business and employment can be taken to be uncertainty about the future. Investment decisions must be made with only limited information, and as more information comes in, the value of those investments will fluctuate. Since that is the source of the fluctuations, business will go up and down in a generally random way. The cycles that seem to be there when we look at charts of business fluctuations will be mostly optical illusions.

The Great Depression

What happened after 1929? Can the story I am telling be applied to the 1930s? To a large extent, I think it can, though I'm not sure exactly where the investment decisions of the 1920s went wrong.

Perhaps it was something like an expectation that the economy had the ability to produce a huge quantity and variety of goods and services.

So people planned on both producing and buying fancy houses, furniture, appliances, cars, food, and more special things. It turned out, however, that the economy did not have this capacity. People had to spend within a smaller budget, so many things that firms had geared up to produce were not in demand. There was a large drop in the value of both human and business capital.

There was one other factor that may have made the depression worse, though. According to Miller and Upton, in the book mentioned above, the price level fell by nearly 50 percent between the end of 1929 and the start of 1933. That's three years. With the price level falling that rapidly, any positive dollar interest rate would represent a rather large interest rate in real terms. Since people could always hold currency, the dollar interest rate couldn't really become negative. So the economy may have been unable to reach its natural equilibrium. The natural equilibrium was bad enough, but the one the economy was forced into was undoubtedly even worse.

References

Miller, Merton and Upton, Charles 1974: *Macroeconomics: A Neoclassical Introduction*. Chicago: University of Chicago Press.

7

How Passive Monetary Policy Might Work

Passive monetary policy means supplying the amount of money that the private sector wants at all times. It means making money freely available in exchange for assets of equal value. If monetary policy is passive, then changes in the stock of money are caused by changes in the public's demand for money, and are not influenced by such things as open market operations.

If monetary policy is passive, then changes in the price level or the rate of inflation must be caused by non-monetary forces, such as changes in the general level of economic activity or changes in the direction and level of government intervention in the foreign exchange market. The demand for money will depend on the price level and the rate of inflation, so there will be a relation between money and prices. But the causation will run from prices to money rather than from money to prices.

Similarly, passive monetary policy will imply a relation between income and money, and a relation between wealth and money. But the causation will run from income or wealth to money rather than the other way around.

With passive monetary policy, an increase in nominal interest rates will mean a decrease in the money stock, other things equal, because an increase in interest rates implies a reduced demand for money. It may look like restrictive monetary policy causing an increase in interest rates, but actually the causation will be just the reverse.

With passive monetary policy, a helicopter dropping currency all around will have little effect. People will pick up the currency and deposit it or exchange it for other assets of equal value. Ultimately, the government will get the currency back. There may be an increase in the amount of government debt outstanding or a reduction in private assets held by the government, but there won't be any significant change in the money stock.

That's what passive monetary policy is. Note that it has nothing to do with steady growth in the money stock. Indeed, steady growth in the money stock is inconsistent with passive monetary policy, because demand for money just doesn't grow steadily. For example, money demand is always high in December for the holiday season, relative to other months of the year.

Does passive monetary policy imply an accelerating flow of money into the private sector, along with an accelerating rate of inflation? Hardly. The demand for money is strictly limited by the fact that it pays no interest, or interest at effective rates lower than market rates of interest on bonds and bills. Passive monetary policy requires that an individual or firm give up assets of equal value to get money. Such exchanges make sense only if the money received will be turning over. They will not go on indefinitely.

Similarly, freely available reserves will not make banks go on a lending spree. An individual bank, if it is behaving optimally, will always be creating demand deposits until the last dollar of demand deposit it creates costs an amount equal to the federal funds rate or some similar rate. If the bank creates more demand deposits than that, it will be losing money. Free availability of reserves will not affect this decision rule for a bank. In fact, for an individual bank, reserves are freely available whether or not monetary policy is passive.

It turns out that there are many ways for a government to adopt a passive monetary policy. With some, it will be obvious that monetary policy is passive. With others, monetary policy can be passive even though the world believes that it is being used actively to influence economic activity, employment, and inflation.

Free Exchange of Reserves and Securities

One way the government can make monetary policy passive is to stand ready to exchange currency or reserves freely for government securities. It can offer to buy or sell government securities at prices that give them interest rates comparable to rates on other securities with the same features.

In principle, the same thing can be done with private securities. The government might accumulate some private securities, and then start exchanging them freely for currency or reserves at market prices.

If the Federal Reserve System is in charge of trading reserves and securities, but insists on following an active monetary policy, then the

Treasury can offset what the Federal Reserve System does. For example, the Treasury can vary the amounts of bills offered at its weekly auctions. If it offers more bills than needed to cover maturing securities and the government deficit, it will be absorbing reserves. If it offers fewer bills, it will be supplying reserves. Either the Treasury or the Federal Reserve System can make monetary policy passive without the cooperation of the other.

The price at which securities are bought or sold is a key variable. I have said that the government can exchange reserves and securities at market prices. That means at the price that the security would have if the government were not buying or selling it. If the government is buying or selling the security, it may be hard to know what the market price would otherwise be. The government can fix the price of any individual security at any level it wants by offering to buy or sell unlimited quantities at that price.

In principle, though, it is possible for the government to offer to exchange reserves or currency and securities at the security prices that would exist if the government didn't try to change those prices. If there is only one kind of security involved, there will be only one price consistent with equilibrium and a given total of net government liabilities. More on that later.

Free Borrowing of Reserves

Another way to reach passive monetary policy is to allow the private sector (perhaps mainly the banks) to borrow reserves freely at something like a market interest rate. The discount window can allow passive monetary policy even when open market operations seem consistent with active monetary policy. So long as there are substantial borrowed reserves, the banks can fully offset open market operations by adding to or subtracting from their borrowings from the Federal Reserve System.

We can see the algebra of this by writing TR for total reserves, BR for borrowed reserves, and NR for non-borrowed reserves. We have:

$$TR = BR + NR. \tag{7.1}$$

Now TR can be given by the private sector's demand for currency and reserves, where the demand for reserves depends on the public's demand for deposits of various kinds. At the same time, NR may be fixed by the government, using open market operations or variations in Treasury offerings of securities. These two are consistent because it takes both TR and NR to determine BR.

$$BR = TR - NR. \tag{7.2}$$

If there are substantial borrowed reserves, it's clear that the government can't force more reserves onto the market by buying securities or by not issuing new securities to replace maturing government securities. Any reserves the government puts out can be returned through repayment of loans.

If some banks have no borrowings, then the government also cannot easily take reserves out of the market. If it tries, then the banks that have not borrowed can do so, and can lend the reserves they get to the banks that lost reserves to the government. Only by putting quotas on all or most banks can the government stop the use of variations in borrowed reserves to offset open market operations.

So it is hard for the government to stop the use of borrowed reserves to make monetary policy passive, and it is easy for the government to allow the use of borrowed reserves to make monetary policy passive. Again, though, we have the question of the interest rate.

Roughly speaking, the interest rate for such borrowing should be a market rate. If the rate is too low, the private sector will keep borrowing and the government will have to issue securities at a great rate to get the money to lend. If the rate is too high, banks will be reluctant to borrow reserves, and we may not get passive monetary policy. The correct rate will make a bank indifferent between buying government securities and paying off some of its loan from the government.

The Right Targets

Yet another way to have passive monetary policy while appearing to use active monetary policy is to use the right targets. For example, suppose that the government watches net free reserves (or its negative, net borrowed reserves). When net free reserves goes up, the government may sell securities in the open market, and when net free reserves goes down, it may buy.

If the government keeps bringing net free reserves back to a target level in this way, then it will essentially be responding to changes in the demand for money. When the public wants more demand deposits, the banks create them, and the added required reserves will cause net free reserves to fall. When the government buys securities in response to this, the banks will have the reserves they need to support the new level of demand deposits without any change in the final value of net free reserves. Monetary policy will be passive.

Interest rate targets can be used in the same way. If the central bank sets interest rate targets that are about equal to what interest rates would be without any active buying or selling of securities, then the buying and selling it does to reach these targets will amount to a passive response to shifts in the demand for currency and reserves.

If all else fails, the central bank can cite "technical factors" as the reason for responding to a shift in demand. Or it can point to unusual events, such as bank failures or defaults on supposedly safe securities, as the reasons for deviating from its usual active monetary policy.

Indirect Methods

All the methods of reaching passive monetary policy given above still do not exhaust the possibilities. For example, the government and the private sector are constantly making payments to one another. If one or the other wants to get rid of currency or reserves, it can use them in making payments. There are so many opportunities to adjust the stock of base money with payments like these that it's hard to see how monetary policy can be anything but passive.

And finally, the government can use fixed exchange rates or intervention under a floating rate system as a way of supplying the currency and reserves that the private sector wants. If the government stands ready to exchange its currency freely (at a certain exchange rate) for the currency of another country, then domestic residents can easily adjust their holdings of currency and reserves.

If the private sector wants more currency, it can sell assets abroad for foreign currency, and then exchange the foreign currency for domestic currency. If the foreign country's monetary policy is passive, this will make the home country's monetary policy passive too.

Free Exchange of Reserves and Deposits

All of the methods mentioned above can be used with existing laws and institutions. There are others, though, that can be used if the government wants to admit that its monetary policy is passive.

For example, the government might set up its interest-bearing liabilities in the form of Federal Reserve Bank deposits rather than

Treasury securities. There might be no government bonds, notes, or bills at all. Instead, the Federal Reserve Banks might accept deposits from individuals, financial institutions, or non-financial firms that pay interest at market rates. These deposits might be like savings accounts, where daily interest is paid and the money can be withdrawn on demand.

The government might still have non-interest-bearing deposits called reserves, and it might still have reserve requirements for deposits at banks. But it could make monetary policy clearly passive by allowing free exchange of currency or reserves for interest-bearing deposits.

Free exchange of currency and deposits means simply that the government will always accept currency for credit to an interest-bearing account, and will always allow withdrawals of currency from an interest-bearing account. If the government had its debt in the form of interest-bearing deposits like this, it's hard to imagine any other policy. How could the government refuse a deposit of currency?

Again, though, we have to worry about the interest rate. In this case it's the interest rate on deposits rather than the interest rate on government securities. Does the interest rate on deposits take the place of the supply of base money as a tool of monetary policy?

No. The interest rate on government deposits must be set passively too. There is only one interest rate at which the public will be willing to hold the accumulated stock of government liabilities. This is an equation that is often omitted from models of the financial sector.

Let's write R for the interest rate on interest-bearing deposits, $D(R)$ for the demand for the interest-bearing deposits as a function of the interest rate, $C(R)$ for the demand for currency and reserves as a function of the interest rate on deposits, and L for the total stock of government liabilities. The total stock of government liabilities can be thought of as fixed at a point in time. It changes as the government runs budget deficits or surpluses, and it can change through gifts or exchange of government liabilities for private assets. But at any point in time, the demand for total government liabilities must equal the total stock of such liabilities. We must have:

$$D(R) + C(R) = L. \qquad (7.3)$$

This equation determines the interest rate on government deposits, and the division of government liabilities between interest-bearing deposits and the sum of currency and reserves. The interest rate is not free to move to make people happy with higher or lower levels of currency plus reserves.

8

What a Non-Monetarist Thinks

I believe that in a country like the US, with a smoothly working financial system, the government does not, cannot, and should not control the money stock in any significant way. The government does, can only, and should simply respond passively to shifts in the private sector's demand for money. Monetary policy is passive, can only be passive, and should be passive. The pronouncements and actions of the Federal Reserve Board on monetary policy are a charade. The Board's monetary actions have almost no effect on output, employment, or inflation.

There aren't many of us around these days. There's only one other person I know of who takes a position almost as strong as mine. There were lots of non-monetarists in eighteenth-century England, but they are gone. The most common positions these days are exemplified by Friedman and Keynes. Friedman believes that monetary policy is a very effective tool for controlling the economy: so powerful that it is more likely to be used badly than to be used well. He recommends a steady growth in the money stock.

Keynes believed, and many living economists seem to believe, that both monetary and fiscal policy are powerful tools for doing good or evil in the economy. They believe in monetary ease, monetary restraint, tax cuts, deficit spending, and trying to get consumers to spend more when the economy seems to have slack. Some of these people even believe that wage and price controls, properly applied at the right times, will have magical restorative effects on the economy.

I don't agree with either of these positions. I don't think any aggregate government policies have much of an impact on the economy. But while some of these policies have at least modest effects of some sort, monetary policy has almost no effect at all. Monetary policy might as well not be formulated.

What the Government Can't Do

I believe that, so long as financial markets are working smoothly, the government cannot control the money stock. If one arm of the government gives the private sector base money that it doesn't want, another arm of the government must be taking back an equal amount.

If the government doesn't control the money stock, then it can't control the economy in any way through control of the money stock. It can't control the price level or the rate of inflation. It can't make individuals spend more or spend less on current consumption. It can't change the interest rates that firms use in making investment decisions, or the level of the stock market, so it can't change investment decisions either. Since the government can't control consumption or investment, it certainly can't control anything that we might call "aggregate demand." And the level of employment or unemployment will change in ways that have nothing to do with government monetary policy.

What the Government Can Do

One thing the government can do is to use a monetary policy that is actually passive without seeming to be passive. The Federal Reserve System can allow variations in borrowed reserves to offset its open market operations, so that total reserves are supplied passively. The Treasury can vary its securities offerings to offset Federal Reserve open market operations that don't fit passive monetary policy. Or the Federal Reserve can simply use open market operations only to keep a target like net borrowed reserves in line.

The government might also adopt an openly passive monetary policy. It might say that monetary policy is not being used to try to influence the economy, and that it stands ready to exchange currency or reserves and government securities freely at prices that reflect market interest rates.

While the government can't control the amount of credit in the economy through open market operations, it can control the amount of borrowing and lending in other ways. Reserve requirements act like a tax on lending in the form of bank deposits. Taxes on interest income are not always fully offset by the deductibility of interest expense. Margin requirements are effective for some investors, and thus prevent some borrowing and lending that would otherwise have been done. Usury laws and deposit rate ceilings interfere with borrowing and lending when the natural borrowing and lending rates are above the ceilings. Both laws and rules prohibit certain kinds of loans by financial institutions that are thought to be too risky. All of these things restrict the amount of credit in the economy.

Restricting credit is the same as restricting borrowing, and restricting borrowing is the same as restricting lending. The effects of restrictions on borrowing are to put a premium on securities and investments that have built-in leverage. High-risk securities have higher prices and lower expected returns than they would otherwise have; low-risk securities have lower prices and higher expected returns than they would otherwise have. Risky real investments are encouraged, while safe real investments are discouraged. Any changes in the restrictions on credit will cause changes in the relative prices of high- and low-risk securities. Note, though, that none of this is the sort of thing the government says it is doing when it varies the restrictions on credit.

Another thing the government can do is to vary the structure of interest rates. In some ways, this is analogous to what it can do to vary the structure of expected returns on risky securities by varying its controls on credit. The government cannot raise or lower interest rates generally, but it can raise some and lower others.

For example, the government can set rates on Treasury bills that are lower than normal by selling relatively small quantities. They will tend to be bought by people who have limited alternatives in the short run. But the government will have to offset this by offering other Treasury securities at higher-than-normal interest rates so that the outstanding government debt will continue to be financed.

If the government continues to try to set short-term rates low and long-term rates high, it will find that its short-term securities are held by fewer and fewer investors, while its long-term securities have to take up the slack. "Institutional factors" and "inertia" can allow the government to move the rates quite far before demand for the low-rate securities is close to zero, and before demand for the high-rate securities exceeds the supply. The government will lose money in this operation, though, so it may not want to keep it going too long.

Similarly, the government can change interest rates on private securities by buying or selling them, but it must at the same time move rates on public securities in the opposite direction. It can sell government bonds at low prices to get the money to buy private bonds at artificially high prices.

It's popular now to talk about the government's effect on the federal funds rate. Again, the government can move that rate, but only by moving some other rate in the opposite direction. If the government offers to lend the banks unlimited amounts on a one-day basis at 2 percent, then the federal funds rate won't be able to get much above 2 percent, and other short-term rates will be affected too. But the government may find itself making massive loans, and having to issue enormous amounts of government securities at higher-than-market rates to get the money for these loans. Since the government will lose by the spread between its borrowing and lending rates, it's not likely to keep this up.

Strangely, all this means that the government can control the stock of any particular kind of interest-bearing government liability. It can make the stock of Treasury bills go down by offering low rates, so long as it offsets that by increasing the stock of some other kind of interest-bearing government liability. It is only the stock of non-interest-bearing government liabilities that the government can't control. And that's because the government doesn't control the interest rate on such liabilities.

Actually, of course, fooling around with the interest rates on various kinds of government securities does have some effect on the private sector's demand for money. So this sort of activity does give the government an indirect way to influence the money stock. But it would not give the government any significant control over important economic matters, so we would still think of monetary policy as passive.

What would happen if the government decided it just wouldn't be passive, and started pulling or pushing on the money supply without letting up? Something would clearly have to give. The financial system would break down in some way. One possibility is hyperinflation, where financial markets are simply not in equilibrium, and it would be unfair to say that an individual is happy with his asset holdings at any point in time (if he holds any money). Another possibility is a "two-price system," where prices in terms of the currency that the government is manipulating differ from prices in terms of other currencies. This is rather common, as when paper currencies trade at a discount in terms of gold, or when currency that can be used for foreign investment trades at a premium relative to currency that can't.

What Does Move the Money Stock?

If the government doesn't directly influence the money stock, what does?

All the factors that affect the demand for money affect the money stock. For example, increasing dollar income and consumption generally means an increasing demand for money. This will be true whether the increase comes from higher real income or higher prices.

Higher wealth may be one factor that leads to higher consumption, and an increase in the level of the stock market generally means higher wealth. So we may find that the money stock goes up when the stock market goes up.

Other things equal, higher nominal interest rates mean a higher cost of holding money, and thus a lower money stock. At least this is true of currency and other components of the money stock that don't bear interest at market rates. If demand deposit interest rates are not restricted, then demand deposits may be unaffected by changes in interest rates.

Some Reasons for Thinking This Way

Why am I a non-monetarist? My reasons are mostly theoretical rather than empirical. In fact, they almost have to be theoretical, because I haven't been able to think of any empirical test, short of using the Federal Reserve System for experiments, that would show whether I'm right or some other school is right.

The basic problem with existing theory is that I have never seen a model of a monetary economy that was consistent with the notion that markets are in continual equilibrium and that expectations are formed rationally, and that allowed for the government to control the money stock. All the models I have seen imply that someone with the model will be able to make profits at the expense of the people whose actions are being modelled. At best, such a model contains the seeds of its own destruction.

I have tried to build such models myself, and I have read about many attempts by others to build such models. Some have tried to say that "imperfections" like costs of information and trading costs justify the assumption that monetary policy can be active. But they have never succeeded in building a sensible model in which these imperfections are included as an integral part of the model, and in which there are no profit opportunities in the light of these imperfections.

My trouble is that I keep thinking about people's budget equations. I think about the fact that outstanding government liabilities must be financed in one form or another. And I think about the fact that what people plan to save and what they plan to spend must add up to what they have.

This means that if a helicopter did go around dropping money, there would normally be no force tending to drive up prices. First, people would want to trade most of their money for interest-bearing assets. (See above for what happens if they can't do that.) Second, they may under some conditions feel wealthier. But suppose they do? Suppose they use part of their perceived wealth to increase consumption. Will that drive up prices?

I think not. The economy produces both consumption goods and investment goods. If demand for consumption goods goes up, demand for investment goods must go down. It's the budget equation again. People know how much output the economy has. They know that if they take more in consumption goods they must take less in investment goods. An increase in consumption may mean a modest increase in consumption goods prices and a modest decrease in investment goods prices, as the economy shifts its output to one from the other. But it won't mean a general increase in prices.

The Currency Trap

As a postscript, let me note that even in my world, there's a problem that can occur when nominal interest rates get too low. It is similar to something called the "liquidity trap" in the world of Keynes.

It happens when the natural level of the nominal interest rate is negative, which usually means that prices are falling at a fairly rapid pace. So long as there is currency around, though, nominal interest rates can't become negative. Who would hold a private or government bond with a negative interest rate if she could hold currency instead? There's no reason why a bond with a zero coupon can't sell at a premium, which means a negative interest rate.

But currency can't do anything similar because it doesn't have a maturity date.

If the natural level of the nominal interest rate goes negative, something must give. I'm not sure what it will be. Maybe the value of real investments will fall and we'll get lots of unemployment. It's even possible that the currency trap played a role in making the Depression worse than it would otherwise have been.

9

Global Monetarism in a World of National Currencies

Introduction

The theory called "global monetarism" or "the monetary approach to the balance of payments" generally assumes that it is not necessary to distinguish between the currencies of different countries.[1] With fixed exchange rates, this theory says, an increase in any one country's money stock will cause a world increase in prices (at least in the long run) by increasing the world's money stock. The size of the effect on world money and prices will depend on the size of the country that increases its money stock relative to the sizes of the other countries.[2]

This theory is based on the notion that money is like gold: it has no national identity. In fact, though, the vast bulk of the money now used in the world does have national identity and is not backed in any meaningful sense by gold or an international paper money.

The usual theory of global monetarism assumes that each country's money stock is partly domestic currency and partly international reserves. It assumes that the total money stock used within a country is related in a stable way to its price level, and that countries influence one another largely through flows of international reserves across national boundaries. In some cases, these flows of international reserves will be in exchange for goods or capital.

I would like to explore the form this theory would take if it were assumed that national currencies are the only kinds of money in the world. Let's look at two models: first, a simple model in which a country's currency is used only internally; and second, a model with international reserves in the sense that one country's currency is held by the governments of other countries.

Reprinted with permission from the *Columbia Journal of World Business*, Spring, 1978.

A Simple Model

To start, we make the simplest and most extreme assumptions consistent with the notion that national currencies are the only kinds of money. They are as follows:

1 Currency is the only form of money. It represents all non-interest-bearing forms of money that may be used in a country.
2 A country's currency is used only internally. The working balances of other countries' currencies that importers and exporters may hold will be ignored.
3 The ratio of a country's price level and the amount of its currency in circulation is constant. In other words, the simplest form of the quantity theory of money is assumed.
4 The exchange rate between two countries is the inverse of the ratio of the price levels in the two countries. The simplest form of purchasing power parity is thus assumed.
5 Monetary policy is used to keep all exchange rates constant through time; this is a world of permanently fixed exchange rates.

Under these assumptions, monetary policy alone is sufficient to fix exchange rates. Two countries need only set the ratio of their money stocks equal to the inverse of the desired exchange rate. No international reserves are needed to set exchange rates. No intervention in foreign exchange markets is needed either.

Since there are no flows of international reserves between countries, it is hard to see how one can meaningfully define a balance-of-payments surplus or deficit. Any country can keep its exchange rate fixed with any other country using monetary policy alone, as long as the two countries have consistent objectives. (It isn't possible for one country to achieve one exchange rate while the other achieves a different exchange rate.) A country would never be forced by international flows to change its target exchange rate with another country.

The changes in a country's price level that go along with keeping exchange rates fixed may come to be regarded as politically unacceptable, so it might devalue or revalue its currency. And if monetary policy affects a country other than through its price level, the country might well decide to change the target exchange rate from time to time. But a devaluation would never be forced by continuing payments deficits.

Home Countries and Target Countries

Let's call a country that chooses its monetary policy to fix its exchange rate with another country a "home country," and a country that chooses its monetary policy in some other way a "target country." If exchange rates are fixed among a group of *n* countries, then it is natural for one of these countries to be a target country and for the remaining *n* − 1 countries to be home countries.

For example, in figure 9.1 we have eight ways for exchange rates to be fixed among five countries. Each country at the start of an

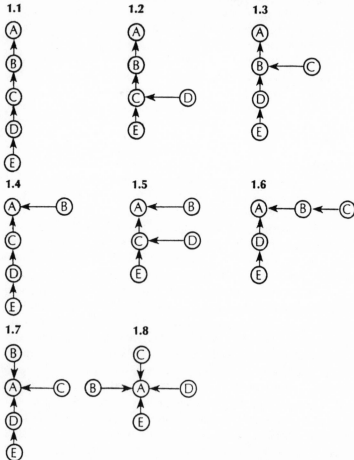

Figure 9.1 Equivalent ways to fix exchange rates

arrow chooses its money stock to keep the desired exchange rate with the country at the other end of the arrow. In section 1.5, for example, countries B and C both fix their exchange rates with country A, while countries D and E both fix their exchange rates with country C.

Sections 1.1 through 1.8 represent equally good ways of fixing exchange rates among five countries, and they all have country A as the target country and the other four countries as home countries. No arrows start with country A, so it may choose its money stock and price level freely.

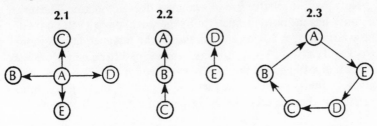

9.2 Unlikely ways to fix exchange rates

Figure 9.2 shows some less likely ways of fixing exchange rates among five countries. Section 2.1 indicates that country A is trying to choose its money stock to fix exchange rates with each of the other four countries. This will be impossible unless the other four countries co-ordinate their policies, which would mean more arrows in the diagram.

The pattern in section 2.2 also won't allow exchange rates to be fixed among five countries. There is nothing in the diagram that would fix rates between the two groups, A, B, and C, on the one hand, and D and E, on the other.

The diagram in section 2.3 will work only if the exchange rates are chosen to be consistent. Every country in 2.3 is a home country; no country has the freedom to set its money stock and price level. It would seem better to erase one of the arrows and make one country a target country, as in 1.1.

It certainly is possible to imagine that the target country shares its power with the home countries, in the sense that it takes into account their suggestions on how it should control its money stock and price level. The home countries have some power to have their suggestions taken seriously, because they are free to stop maintaining the customary exchange rates if they are not happy with the target country's policies. As long as fixed rates are maintained, there is just one degree of freedom among the monetary policies in the *n* countries.[3]

In other words, with given exchange rates, one country is free to choose its money stock and price level, while all the others must follow its lead. Through fixed exchange rates, the target country chooses every other country's price level and money stock along with its own.

In the literature on global monetarism, "fixed exchange rates" generally mean that no country has direct control over its money stock.[4] In our simple model, we see that a target country does have direct control over its money stock, in the sense that it can use control of its money stock toward objectives other than fixing exchange rates.

Note that the relative size of a country does not matter. The target country has the power to determine the world price level, no matter how large it is. A 10 percent increase in the target country's money stock will cause a 10 percent increase in every other country's money stock and a 10 percent increase in every country's price level. What gives a country power is the fact that it's not trying to fix exchange rates, not the fact that it's a big part of the world economy.[5]

International Reserves

Now let us turn to a more complex model, in which one country is an issuer of international reserves, which means that other countries' governments may choose to hold inventories of the issuer's currency. The country issuing international reserves is the "issuer," or the "reserve currency country."

The issuer may be either a target country or a home country. The fact that its currency is held by other countries gives it no more power to control money supplies and price levels than it had before. If it is a target country, it already had that power. If it is a home country, it has no more power than it had before. It must sterilize flows of reserves across its borders if it is to maintain fixed exchange rates.

In other words, a country does not gain any control over its own or the world's money stock by becoming an issuer of international reserves. Thus, this model is in contrast to the literature on world monetarism, where a reserve currency country is thought to have additional control over the world money stock and price level.[6]

Any home country must sterilize flows of reserves across its borders if it is to maintain fixed exchange rates. But a home country does have the freedom to eliminate reserve flows across its borders by holding constant its inventory of international reserves. If there are no reserve flows, no sterilization will be needed.

No country gains any control over its money supply, price level, or exchange rates by becoming a holder of international reserves. A target country controls money supplies and price levels already, and a home country controls its exchange rate already. If a country becomes a holder of international reserves, it loses interest on the currency it holds, which shows up as seigniorage gains to the issuer.

Thus, no country gains by holding international reserves, and every country other than the issuer loses by the amount of the interest sacrificed on its inventory of reserves. So it seems natural for every country to set its holdings of international reserves at zero. That leads back to the simple model discussed above.

Whether international reserves are held or not, the important distinction is between target country and home country, rather than between large country and small country or between issuer and holder of international reserves.

Conclusions

Neither of the models explored in this chapter is an accurate description of the way the international economy has worked or could work, because their assumptions just aren't realistic. My main objective has been to show some of the changes that need to be made in existing models of global monetarism if they are to be applied to a world of fixed exchange rates with national currencies only.

I expect, however, that some of the features of these models will be maintained when the assumptions are relaxed to make the models more realistic. The following may continue to be true:

1 Intervention is not needed to fix exchange rates; monetary policy alone is enough. Monetary policy is ineffective for any other purpose in a country that is actively fixing exchange rates, so it might as well be used as a substitute for intervention.

2 International reserves are not needed to fix exchange rates. A country can use monetary policy or it can use international reserves for intervention, combined with a policy of exchanging capital or bonds for reserves to keep inventories of international reserves near zero. Thus, reserve flows will never force devaluation or revaluation of a currency.

3 The kind of country that has the power to control money supplies and price levels when exchange rates are fixed is the target

country, a country not active in fixing exchange rates. A 10 percent increase in the target country's money stock means a 10 percent increase in the world price level. The size of the target country and whether it is an issuer of international reserves do not matter.

I am grateful to Robert Aliber, Stanley Black, Rudiger Dornbusch, Stanley Fischer, Arthur Laffer, Merton Miller, Ronald McKinnon, Michael Mussa, and a referee for helpful comments on earlier versions of this chapter.

Notes

1 The term "global monetarism" is used in a comprehensive survey of the relevant literature by Whitman (1975, pp. 491–536). See also Frenkel and Johnson (1976). Another survey of the theory is provided by Kemp (1975, pp. 14–22). Perhaps the best-known paper on "the monetary approach to the balance of payments," which has appeared in several versions, is Johnson's (1972, pp. 1555–72). The basic theory is restated by Swoboda (1973, pp. 136–54). The theoretical framework used in these two papers was developed in part by Mundell (1971).

2 For example, Whitman (1975, p. 523) says that the US can control its own money stock because of its size; Courchene (1973, p. 70) says that a country large enough to have some impact on world prices can influence both domestic and world money stocks; Frenkel and Johnson (1976, pp. 21–45) say that a country's control over the world money stock depends on its size (p. 26); and Humphrey (1976, pp. 13–22) says that a country's control over its own money stock depends on its size.

3 Johnson (1973, pp. 181–6) makes this point in a context involving both monetary and fiscal policy instruments.

4 Whitman (1975, p. 494) says that one of the propositions of global monetarism is this: "Any exercise of monetary policy to change the domestic component of the monetary base will, under fixed exchange rates, be offset by an equal and opposite change in the foreign component of that base." Frenkel and Johnson (1976, p. 6) say, "Under a fixed exchange rate the supply of money in any country is endogenous."

5 This contrasts with the literature on global monetarism cited in note 2.

6 Whitman (1975, p. 524) says that the United States can control its own money stock partly because it is a reserve currency country. Frenkel and Johnson (1976, p. 26) make the same point about a country whose national money is internationally acceptable.

This entire chapter was written under the assumption that active monetary policy is possible. I didn't and don't believe it is possible. I was simply trying to show some of the contradictions in a particular kind of monetarism.

References

Courchene, Thomas J. 1973: The price-specie-flow mechanism and the gold exchange standard: some exploratory empiricism relating to the endogeneity of country money balances. In Harry G. Johnson and Alexander K. Swoboda (eds), *The Economics of Common Currencies*, Cambridge: Harvard University Press, 70.

Frenkel, Jacob A. and Johnson, Harry G. 1976: *The Monetary Approach to the Balance of Payments*. Toronto: University of Toronto Press.

Humphrey, Thomas M. 1976: A monetarist model of world inflation and the balance of payments. *Economic Review*, Federal Reserve Bank of Richmond, 62, 13–22.

Johnson, Harry G. 1972: The monetary approach to balance of payments theory. *Journal of Financial and Quantitative Analysis*, 7, 1555–72.

Johnson, Harry G. 1973: *Further Essays in Monetary Economics*. Cambridge: Harvard University Press.

Kemp, Donald S. 1975: A monetary view of the balance of payments. *Federal Reserve Bank of St Louis Review*, 57, 14–22.

Mundell, Robert A. 1971: *Monetary Theory*. Pacific Palisades: Goodyear.

Swoboda, Alexander K. 1973: Monetary policy under fixed exchange rates: effectiveness, the speed of adjustment, and proper use. *Economica*, 40, 136–54.

Whitman, Marina V. N. 1975: Global monetarism and the monetary approach to the balance of payments. *Brookings Papers on Economic Activity*, March, 491–536.

10

The ABCs of Business Cycles

Business cycle peaks occur when there is a good match between the types of skills or physical capital wanted in an economy and the types of skills or physical capital available; conversely, troughs occur when wants and skills are poorly matched. The business cycle is largely a matter of choice. That is, the level of business cycle fluctuations reflects the trade-offs people face between (A) expected growth, (B) fluctuations in output, and (C) unemployment.

The conventional explanations for fluctuations in output and unemployment all imply that there are unexploited profit opportunities in the world. They cannot hold true in an economy that is in continual equilibrium, where people are constantly seeking profit opportunities.

A more rational explanation for business cycles may be found in shifting demand and supply curves. Shifting tastes and shifting technology lead to wage differentials between different sectors of the economy. These will lead to unemployment as people move from low-wage sectors in search of jobs in high-wage sectors. Unemployment in the form of job layoffs – whether short-term or indefinite – occurs when differentials exist between current and future labor productivity.

The average severity of a society's business cycles is largely a matter of choice. If people chose to invest in sectors with both high and low expected growth, the economy would be more diversified and exhibit lower fluctuations in output, but also lower growth, than it would if people invested only or primarily in sectors with high growth. Investments in sectors that do not move together will allow greater diversification, hence lower fluctuations; but sectors that move together will generate lower unemployment, since wage differentials will be smaller.

Reprinted with permission from *Financial Analysts Journal*, November/December, 1981. All rights reserved. *Copyright©* The Financial Analysts Federation, 1981.

In this sense, forecasts of business cycle movements will not help in formulating countercyclical fiscal and monetary policies. The level of business cycle fluctuations we have is the level we want, given the trade-offs people face between (A) expected growth, (B) fluctuations in output, and (C) unemployment.

Nor will predictions of business cycle movements help in predicting stock price movements. On the other hand, stock market movements can be used to predict business cycle movements. For example, large moves in opposite directions in different sectors of the stock market should be followed, normally, by an increase in unemployment.

People and firms are constantly seeking profit opportunities and trying to take advantage of the ones they find. They try to buy low and sell high. They try to make investments in business that will end up with a value greater than cost. They look for high expected returns.

People also want to reduce risk. An investment that earns one percentage point more than the interest rate (on average) will be unattractive if it has as much risk as the market. People want three things:

A high expected return,
B low risk, and
C high value.

Of course, they can't generally have all the ABCs at once. There are trade-offs. High expected return generally goes with high risk, or with low value. When people are relatively averse to risk, they will choose low risk and low expected return; when they are relatively tolerant of risk, they will choose high risk and high expected return. When people value the present more than the future, they will choose high value and low expected return; when they value the future more, they will choose low value and high expected return.

Looking for profit opportunities is costly; so are the steps needed to take advantage of profit opportunities that are found. It's costly to convert a plant from producing something that's in less demand to producing something that's in more demand. It's costly for an individual to leave one job in search of a job that pays more. It's costly to obtain government approval to undertake certain ventures. My economic models include these costs, either explicitly or implicitly; I assume that individuals and firms look for opportunities that are still profitable after these costs are taken into account.[1]

In my models, markets work. Prices and wages are generally free to move, barring government interference. People and goods are free to move, so long as the adjustment costs are paid. Investment decisions are made rationally, though some investments may turn out badly. People make mistakes, but they don't make the same mistakes over and over. The economy is in continual equilibrium.

What are Business Cycles?

Business cycles are fluctuations in economic activity. Business cycles show up in virtually all measures of economic activity – output, income, employment, unemployment, retail sales, new orders by manufacturers; even housing starts. When times are good, they tend to be good all over; and when times are bad, they tend to be bad all over. A particular cycle's tendency to affect many sectors and many measures of economic activity in the same direction is called its diffusion; some cycles are more diffuse than others, but there will be an average degree of diffusion that depends on the structure of the economy.

Neither good times nor bad times last forever. On average, economic conditions are neither good nor bad; they're middling. Good times are more likely to get worse than to get better; and bad times are more likely to get better than to get worse. When economic conditions are average, we know only that they won't stay average; at some time in the future they'll be good, and at some time in the future they'll be bad. Of course, in the background, we have normal economic growth: both peaks and troughs tend to get higher over time.

A business cycle can be likened to a slow motion film of a pebble being washed down a sluice with a rough bottom. The motion of the pebble is erratic, but it keeps returning to the center of the sluice, and it keeps moving down. (Of course, for the business cycle, the film would run in reverse, because output tends to rise over time.)

The duration of the pebble's swings will vary greatly. There will be an average time from one swing to the next, but the actual time can differ widely from the average, and the average can change as the construction of the sluice changes. Similarly, business cycles will have some average duration, but the typical cycle will differ greatly from the average of many cycles.

The pebble in the reverse-motion film swings up on both sides of its path, while the business cycle swings up on one side and down on the other side of its path. There will be an average height for the pebble's swings, as there is an average depth for business cycles.

The depth of a single cycle, though, will be subject to many random influences. It's likely to differ significantly from the average business cycle depth.

What happens if we speed up the flow of water in the sluice? The pebble will move more rapidly, and its movements will be more erratic. It may even bounce right out of the sluice. As we will see, society can choose business cycles that correspond to a wide range of water speeds: business cycles with slow growth and small fluctuations, or business cycles with fast growth and large fluctuations. The more tolerant of risk the society's typical person is, the faster the growth and the larger the fluctuations.

What Causes Business Cycles?

When they look at business cycles, economists seem more like priests than scientists. Their theories differ for reasons that seem to be largely historical or accidental. There seem to be few facts from which one can draw definite conclusions. We can classify the generally accepted branches of the church as follows:

A ancient, or the Keynesian theories;
B before, or the monetary theories; and
C current, or the rational expectations theories.

The branches overlap a great deal. The Keynesian theories have monetary elements; the monetary theories allow a role for fiscal policy; the rational expectations theories are really cleaned-up monetary theories. No amount of cleaning, though, can disguise the fact that all these theories are disequilibrium theories. In every one, there is a way for individuals to profit if the world works as the theory says it does.

In Keynesian theories, the interest rate is allowed to differ from the return on low-risk capital. But if that really happened, people could take advantage of it on a massive scale. If the interest rate were below the return on capital, almost everyone would want to borrow to buy capital. If the interest rate were above the return on capital, almost everyone owning capital would want to sell it and invest the proceeds in loans earning the interest rate. Thus the interest rate must be equal to the return on low-risk capital, and this feature of Keynesian theory goes out the window.

Another feature of Keynesian theory that's hard to accept is the notion that people can be unemployed because wages stubbornly refuse to fall when they should. If an individual were willing to work at a low wage, it would be in her interest to let employers know this, and to convince them that she's as good as the next person. It would also be in employers' interest to seek out people who are willing to work at low wages, and to offer to hire them or to lower the wages of workers they already have. Since both parties would have an interest in curing unemployment by letting wages fall, it's hard to see how unemployment due to sticky wages could arise in the first place. Of course, there will always be some unemployment due to union activity, minimum wages, and unemployment benefits, but these aren't the causes of sticky wages the Keynesians have in mind.

In monetary theories, the government can do good or evil through monetary policy. It can cause recessions by using the wrong monetary policy or cure them by using the right monetary policy. In the end, monetarists often decide that attempts to cure recessions using monetary policy are likely to make business cycles worse, so they recommend a predictable monetary policy such as constant rate of growth in the money stock.

Before the current crop of rational expectations theories, monetary theories assumed, in effect, that the government could fool most of the people most of the time. The older theories assumed, for example, that the government could adopt a policy of increasing the rate of money growth in response to signs of an impending recession. Individuals would never figure the policy out, so they would always be surprised at the higher rate of growth. They would increase their spending, and this increased consumer spending would then make the recession milder than it would have been. Does that make sense?

The rational expectations theories get around this problem. These theories assume that individuals will figure out any government policy that can be figured out. People will make errors, but they won't make the same error consistently. But rational expectations theories have problems of their own. They assume that the primary cause of business cycles is uncertainty about current monetary policy. When a person sees demand for his output increase, he's uncertain whether it's a real increase in demand or an increase that reflects the fact he hasn't been raising his prices to keep up with inflation. Just in case it's a real increase in demand, he will increase his output rate somewhat.

In rational expectations theories, an unexpected increase in the money stock leads to an unexpected increase in the price level and a jump in output. Similarly, an unexpected decline in the money stock makes output go down. But if the real effects of random elements in monetary policy were significant, the government could simply announce the current money stock frequently, and the business cycle would mostly go away. Or, if the government refused to do that, some enterprising soul would develop a way of reporting the current price level with little delay and little error. She would profit and so would the rest of us.

So much for the theories currently in vogue. All of them imply that there are great profit opportunities in the world. Anyone understanding the theory would know how to take advantage of these opportunities. So we can't take seriously what they have to say about the causes of business cycles.

In my theory, business cycles are caused in part by shifting tastes and shifting technology – by shifting demand and supply curves. Labor markets provide the simplest example. When demand for shoe machine operators declines and demand for computer operators rises, people will shift out of the first group and into the second. Some people will shift directly, but most of the shifts will be indirect. The people who leave shoe machinery will not be the same as those who go into computers. Some people will shift without a break in employment, but some will be unemployed between jobs. The more shifting there is, the more unemployment there will be.

If the world were static, people would settle into their jobs, and employers would learn about their skills. There would be no reason for employees to want to change jobs and no reason for employers to want them to change. But there are continual changes in people's tastes for consumer goods and services and constant changes in the economy's ability to supply various combinations of goods and services.

Business cycle peaks occur when there is a good match between the types of skills wanted and the types of skills available or between the types of physical capital wanted and the types of physical capital available. Business cycle troughs occur when there is a poor match between wants and skills. The peaks and troughs occur within a path that is itself subject to random influences; new discoveries may shift an economy onto a higher path, while bad weather or war may shift it onto a lower path. These random influences are not always large, either; an accumulation of small shocks will have the same impact as one large shock.

A mismatch will occur when investments in physical or human capital do not pay off as expected or when actual wants turn out to differ from expected wants. Something as simple as the decision to produce a new toy is the raw material of the business cycle. If demand for the toy turns out to be high, or if production costs turn out to be low, that will be good for the economy. If demand for the toy turns out to be low, or if production costs turn out to be high, that will be bad for the economy. The accumulation of these correct and incorrect decisions creates the business cycle. In this sense, the business cycle is due to errors – errors in forecasting tastes or errors in forecasting technology. But these are unavoidable errors; the investment decisions made are the best ones possible in the light of the information available when they are made.

Unemployment is voluntary in the sense that it is a shift from a low-wage sector to a higher wage sector. It's involuntary in the sense that many people making this shift will wish they had made investments earlier that would have put them into higher wage sectors. But at the time they made them, their investments were correct.

Unemployment is not just job search. People who have been laid off and are waiting for recall are also counted as unemployed. They are unemployed because they are worth less to their employers now than they probably will be in the future. They are not willing to work at a wage that would be low enough to induce employers to keep them on the job.

Inflation normally plays no role in this theory. The correct or incorrect allocation of skills to sectors can occur at any rate of inflation. Rapid advances (or retreats) in technology (or tastes) can occur at any rate of inflation. The one exception is when inflation turns negative – when it turns to substantial deflation, as it did in the 1930s. Substantial deflation can make things worse.

What Caused the Great Depression?

According to my theory, we don't fully know what caused the Great Depression. Much of it was due to a mismatch between wants and skills that would be impossible to detail now because we don't have enough data. It was a great stroke of bad luck, wherein a number of factors moved in the wrong way at the same time.

Part of it was an across-the-board decline in technology. Productivity in agriculture had declined, and reciprocal increases in tariffs reduced the productivity of international trade. Part of it was a change in tastes: we may have become less happy with what we could produce across the board, and we may have shifted emphasis from one sector to another. Unemployment rose as people shifted from sectors that were less in demand to sectors that were more in demand and as people decided not to work at all rather than to work at the extremely low wages justified by their productivity in creating the things people wanted.

According to this explanation, as far as it goes, the Great Depression was just like any other downturn, only worse. This may help to explain why the price level started to decline. Once the deflation rate became severe enough that short-term Treasury bill rates fell to zero, another factor came into play – the currency trap.

Treasury bill rates can't fall below zero because, if they were negative, people would hold currency instead of Treasury bills. If currency did not exist, substantial deflation would result in negative interest rates. Since currency does exist, substantial deflation results in zero interest rates on Treasury bills and high positive real interest rates.

How does the economy adjust to high real interest rates from this source? I don't know, but I do know that it will cause great disruptions. Thus the currency trap made the Great Depression more than just a severe recession.

Can We Stop the Business Cycle?

The business cycle is largely a matter of choice. An individual (at least in a non-union job) can avoid being laid off by agreeing to work at substantially less than the going wage for her skill level. She has a lower wage but greater security, because other workers will be laid off first.

Similarly, society can avoid large fluctuations in output by agreeing to lower output and lower expected growth in output. Society can reduce the level of unemployment by making job changes very expensive for the individual and the firm or by subsidizing wages in low-wage sectors and taxing wages in high-wage sectors. This, however, will reduce output and expected growth.

More generally, the choices that the typical individual makes involve the trade-offs discussed in the introduction. The individual wants:

A high expected growth in output,
B small fluctuations in output, and
C low average unemployment.

Since these goals are generally incompatible, the individual must strike a balance. Output fluctuations and unemployment can be sharply reduced, but only at the cost of lower expected growth in output.

Investments in sectors with both high and low expected growth will allow greater diversification, hence lower fluctuations in output, than investments in sectors with high growth only. That's why there's a trade-off between expected growth and fluctuations.

Investments in sectors that may or may not move together will allow greater diversification, hence lower fluctuations in output, than investments in sectors that mostly move together. But sectors that move together will generate lower unemployment, because wage differentials will be smaller on average. When wages are high in one sector, they will be high in most others, and we won't have the movement between sectors that generates unemployment. That's why there's a trade-off between fluctuations and unemployment.

Business cycles are the result of people balancing their interests in A, B, and C. If they were to put less emphasis on A, and more emphasis on B and C, business cycles would be less important. In that sense, business cycles can be stopped. They aren't stopped because people don't want them stopped. The price would be too high.

Can We Stimulate Growth?

The expected rate of growth of consumption is also a matter of choice. An individual can have higher consumption in the future by spending less now and saving more. She can have higher expected growth in consumption by investing in riskier assets or securities.

Similarly, society can increase the expected growth rate of output or consumption by agreeing to less consumption now and greater uncertainty in future consumption. Certain government policies can discourage current consumption and encourage risk-taking; these policies will increase the expected growth rate of consumption. But there is always a price to pay for faster expected growth.

The choices that the typical individual must make will balance:

A high expected growth in consumption,
B small fluctuations in consumption, and
C high current consumption.

Expected growth in consumption can be increased, but only if we increase uncertainty about future consumption or reduce current consumption. The current expected growth rate may well be optimal; in that case, there is no reason to call for an increase in the growth rate.

Of course, it's possible that people are making unenlightened choices, and that there are ways we don't yet know about for improving A, B, and C at the same time. If those ways can be found, we will escape the trade-offs we now face.

Also, it's possible that government policies are distorting individual choices in unnecessary ways. For example, it may be that a change from a tax on income to a tax on spending could be done in a way that would make most people much better off. This change would reduce current consumption but increase the growth rate of consumption.

Can We Predict Business Cycle Movements?

If my model of business cycles is correct, then some aspects of business cycle movements can be predicted with at least some accuracy. If unemployment is unusually high, we can predict a decline; if it is unusually low, we can predict a rise. If unemployment is unusually high, we can predict faster than usual growth in output; if it is unusually low, we can predict slower than usual growth in output. These predictions will be better than those that don't take unemployment into account, but they will still be wrong much of the time.

Forecasts like this are not apt to help in predicting stock market movements because they make use of information that is widely available, hence already discounted. But we can reverse the procedure and use stock market movements to help predict business cycle movements. Again, the predictions will be far from perfect, since the stock market reflects information about many things other than the immediate future of the business cycle. They will, however, be better than predictions that don't use stock market information.

We could also use the behavior of individual sectors of the stock market to predict unemployment. If my theory is correct, large moves in opposite directions in different sectors should be followed, normally, by an increase in unemployment. If the coherence of different sectors of the economy goes down over time, we might expect the average level of unemployment to go up, because wage differentials will tend to increase.

The sector-by-sector behavior of stocks is also useful in predicting sector-by-sector changes in outputs, profits, or investment. When stocks in a given sector go up, more often than not that sector will show a rise in sales, earnings, and outlays for plant and equipment. Again, the resulting predictions are far from perfect, but they are better than predictions that don't make use of stock market data.

Forecasts of business cycle movements are helpful because they tell us what to expect and allow us to adjust our budgets. If my theory is correct, however, forecasts of business cycle movements are not helpful as inputs to the formulation of countercyclical fiscal and monetary policy. The level of business cycle fluctuations we have is the level we want, given the trade-offs we face between (A) expected growth, (B) fluctuations, and (C) unemployment.

Notes

1 One way to seek profit opportunities is via the government. Some activities are normally and properly done by the government, and I generally think of the government as the agent of people in carrying out these activities. Defense is a good example. Governments may be mistaken, but they are rarely malevolent, at least in this country. Government employees may act in their own interest rather than in the interest of the people, but there are ways of controlling them, just as there are ways of controlling managers who don't act in the interest of a firm's stockholders.

11

A Gold Standard with Double Feedback and Near Zero Reserves

If a government can buy and sell gold freely while maintaining a stock of gold equal to a given fraction of its outstanding money stock, then it can adopt a gold standard with near zero reserves that stabilizes the price level. There is feedback from the gold stock to open market operations, and from the price level to the price of gold. The cost of using this method to stabilize the price level would be minimal. Similarly, exchange rates could be maintained indefinitely with near zero reserves, with near zero reserve flows, and with no danger of speculative attack.

Introduction

One hopes, with a gold standard, to set the level of a price index by setting the price of gold.[1]

When a government fixes the price of wheat by agreeing to buy unlimited amounts at a price that is thought to be fair to farmers, the main goal is not to influence the prices of other goods and services. In fact, the relationship goes the other way. When the prices of other goods and services rise, the government is apt to raise the price at which it buys wheat.

When a government fixes the price of oil, and introduces a rationing system to balance supply and demand, the main goal is again not to influence the prices of other goods and services. If other prices rise while the price of oil is not changed, the rationing may have to become more severe and black markets may grow, but there are no obvious forces tending to moderate the rate at which these other prices rise.

The gold standard I will discuss uses a different method for setting the commodity price.[2] In a sense, it is a combination of the wheat

115

method and the oil method. The government stands ready to buy or sell gold freely at a given price, just as the government stands ready to buy wheat freely at a given price. But the government's inventory of gold is fixed by a backing rule, saying that the amount of gold held will be a given fraction of the money stock. One possible backing rule says that the government's stock of gold shall be kept near zero, just as the government's stock of oil can be kept at zero in connection with its method for fixing oil prices.[3]

If the gold standard with an exact backing rule works, then I claim it will work when the rule says the government is to hold almost no reserves at all.

Assumptions

I wish to adopt all the assumptions that Barro (1979) uses.

In his world, gold is supplied from mines at a rate that depends on its relative price. Gold is demanded by the private sector in an amount that depends on its current and future relative prices. Gold is used in both consumer goods and industrial goods, but it is not used in coins.

The government holds a stock of gold equal to a fixed fraction λ of the outstanding stock of money. The government's gold does not depreciate, but the private sector's gold depreciates at a fixed rate δ.

The government buys and sells gold freely at a fixed price P_g. This price may change through time.

Income y affects the demand for money, but is determined by factors outside of the model. There is a fully developed financial system, including currency, banks, stocks, and bonds, in the background.

In addition, Barro assumes implicitly that the government conducts open market operations on the side, to keep its gold stock at the required fixed fraction λ.

Official buying and selling of gold will keep the reserve ratio λ unchanged only when λ is one. When it is less than one, official buying and selling will create the need for further transactions. These transactions can take the form of open market exchanges of bonds and reserves. When the government buys a dollar's worth of gold, it must buy $1/\lambda - 1$ dollars' worth of bonds on the open market to keep the reserve ratio at λ. When it sells gold, it must sell bonds.

When λ is near zero, the government buys and sells almost no gold. Shocks are met almost entirely through open market operations.

Conclusions

In Barro's world, there is always an equilibrium for all variables, including the price level P, for which the price of gold is constant at P_g. (Assuming that the functions he writes down are well-behaved.) Thus a government can never be forced to abandon the gold standard by the factors in Barro's model. If there is such a thing as a "speculative attack," it must come from forces outside of Barro's model.[4]

Moreover, there is a unique equilibrium path for all variables, including the price level P and the money stock. There is no scope for monetary policy within a fixed reserve ratio gold standard. There is only one equilibrium path for the money stock for any given reserve ratio λ. The government must engage in ordinary open market operations that provide this path for the money stock.

Barro (1979, p. 22) notes that the resource cost of the reserves held by the government is an increasing function of λ. This implies that the optimal value of λ is near zero. If the gold standard as Barro describes it will work for any value of λ less than one, it will work for a λ near zero. The government needs only small working inventories of gold.

The process seems especially odd when λ is near zero. In that case, the government meets a decrease in the demand for money, not by selling gold for currency or reserves, but by selling bonds for currency or reserves. If there is an increase in demand for gold, the government will find itself contracting the money supply. This will be associated with a decline in the price level if the price of gold is constant. The government's gold stock will fall only slightly and temporarily.

With λ equal to zero, the gold window is effectively turned into a bond window.

If this argument is correct, then a government can also maintain fixed exchange rates with other governments while maintaining nearly zero reserves. Speculative attacks, if they can succeed at all, must succeed for reasons outside of Barro's model. Within Barro's model, a government can maintain fixed exchange rates indefinitely.

Of course, if every government maintains zero reserves of gold and other currencies, there will be no reserve flows between governments in any sense. This will be true even though each country is permanently on a gold standard, and even though exchange rates are permanently fixed.[5]

Feedback

Open market operations on the side can be governed by a feedback rule. When the government starts to experience an outflow of gold, it can sell bonds for currency or reserves in large enough amounts to reverse the outflow. I see no reason why this response cannot be instantaneous.

The reason for using a gold standard is to stabilize the price level. Since the real price of gold is not constant, the government can use a feedback rule to set the price of gold so that the level of an index of prices of other goods and services will be constant.[6] When the price level starts to rise, the price of gold is dropped; and when the price level starts to fall, the price of gold is raised. The only delays in this process should be due to the time it takes to measure the level of the price index.

Thus one feedback rule operates from the government's gold stock to open market operations, while another operates from the level of a price index to the price of gold. With both feedback rules in operation, it appears that the indirect costs of operating a gold standard would be minimized. Since there would not be any significant moves in the price level, the fact that the money stock might move around a lot would be of no importance.

This kind of gold standard would minimize the direct costs associated with holding a significant inventory of gold, and the indirect costs associated with variations in the price level. The economic costs would be minimal.

If we count as a cost the inability of the government to use expansionary monetary policy, then we can add the price level itself as a policy variable. Under this kind of gold standard, the government can choose any rate of inflation or deflation it wants.

It seems that this kind of gold standard is the one that should be studied by any country thinking of adopting a gold standard.

We don't have to choose between adopting a gold standard and selling the gold stock. We can adopt a gold standard *and* sell most of the gold stock.

I am grateful to Eugene Fama for many useful conversations on these issues, and to Carl Christ, Paul Krugman, and Jurg Niehans for comments on an earlier draft of this chapter.

Notes

1 Fisher (1920) discusses the use of the gold standard to stabilize the price level. Friedman (1951) has a thorough analysis of the economics of several variations on the gold standard, emphasizing countercyclical effects and controls on capricious government policy. Samuelson (1971) looks at a model of the gold standard in which gold itself is used as money.
2 I will work with a model developed by Barro (1979).
3 Hall (1981) discusses another way to fix the price of a commodity without using government inventories of the commodity. The government passes a law that (a) allows buyers to insist on using the commodity at a given price to pay for other goods and services, and (b) allows sellers to insist that buyers use the commodity at the given price to pay for the sellers' goods and services.
4 Salant and Henderson (1978) have a model in which speculative attacks can be effective. Their model appears to apply more to wheat than to gold. They assume there are no transactions on the side. Similarly, Krugman (1979) has a model in which speculative attacks on fixed exchange rates can succeed. He assumes that there are no assets other than currency, so again there can be no transactions on the side. Rather than modelling forces outside of Barro's world, they seem to obtain their results by assuming that the intervention has no apparent economic purpose. Fixing the price of gold without transactions on the side will not fix the level of an index of prices of other goods and services. Their models may be realistic in the sense that countries may sometimes intervene for no apparent economic reason.
5 In such a world, the monetary approach to the balance of payments, as described by Whitman (1975) and in Frenkel and Johnson (1976), would seem to lose its meaning.
6 Fisher (1920) proposes such a feedback rule.

References

Barro, Robert J. 1979: Money and the price level under the gold standard. *Economic Journal*, 89, 13–33.
Fisher, Irving. 1920: *Stabilizing the Dollar*. New York: Macmillan.
Frenkel, Jacob A. and Johnson, Harry G. 1976: *The Monetary Approach to the Balance of Payments*. Toronto: University of Toronto Press.
Friedman, Milton 1951: Commodity-reserve currency. *Journal of Political Economy*, 59, 203–32.

Hall, Robert 1981: Explorations in the gold standard and related policies for stabilizing the dollar. NBER Conference Paper No. 105.

Krugman, Paul 1979: A model of balance-of-payments crises. *Journal of Money, Credit and Banking*, 11, 311–25.

Salant, Stephen W. and Henderson, Dale W. 1978: Market anticipations of government policies and the price of gold. *Journal of Political Economy*, 86, 627–48.

Samuelson, Paul A. 1971: An exact Hume-Ricardo-Marshall model of international trade. *Journal of International Economics*, 1, 1–18.

Whitman, Marina V. N. 1975: Global monetarism and the monetary approach to the balance of payments. *Brookings Papers on Economic Activity*, 3, 491–536.

12

The Trouble with Econometric Models

The trouble with econometric models is that, while they purport to tell us something about causal relations between variables, they almost invariably rely on correlations to imply causation. While correlations can tell us much about how variables are statistically related, they tell us little about how they are causally related. For example, consumption and output show a positive correlation; but an econometric model that assigns a causal role to consumption and one that assigns a passive role to consumption would be equally consistent with the observable correlations. It is doubtful that traditional econometric methods will survive.

In the simplest case, the economic variables of interest obey a joint normal distribution. For any given values of some of the variables, each of the others follows a normal distribution. Many of the problems one encounters in trying to make sense of economic data come from the many ways in which the distribution of the variables can be other than joint normal. The most basic problem, though, is present even when all the variables are random and obey a joint normal distribution. That problem is that of relating correlation and causation.[1]

We will assume, in what follows, that all variables obey a joint normal distribution. The problem of relating correlation and causation is even more difficult in more complex cases, but it is so serious in the simplest case that we do not need to look at the complex cases.

In general, one can analyze data in two ways.[2] A "descriptive analysis" involves summarizing the data in various ways and developing methods for predicting, using purely statistical tools, future values of some of the variables. When the variables obey a joint normal distribution, the data can be summarized using the mean or average level of each variable, the standard deviation or variability of each variable, and the correlations among all pairs of variables. I use the word "correlation" as shorthand for such a summary.

A "structural analysis" involves searching for economic relations among the variables, partly in order to predict how the variables would change if various actions were taken by individuals, firms, or governments. A structural analysis or analysis of the economic relations among the variables is really an analysis of the causal relations among the variables.[3] We want to know what the effects of an individual's, firm's, or government's action will be. In this chapter, an "econometric model" means a model used for structural analysis. Thus, an econometric model is a model of "causation."

One of the basic principles of econometrics is "correlation does not imply causation." There is general agreement on this point when it is stated this way. The problem is that almost every attempt to develop an econometric model seems to make use of correlations in subtle ways to imply causation. Since an econometric model is by definition a causal model, and since regression coefficients are closely related to partial correlation coefficients, the use of regressions to develop or refine an econometric model usually amounts to interpreting correlation as implying causation.

If we are to learn about economics from data, we must make causal inferences. I have done several studies in which I try to infer causality from data.[4] But standard econometric methods do not in themselves allow us to make such inferences. People who do econometric studies often go to great lengths to bring in other information that will tell about causation.[5]

I believe, though, that people have almost always failed in their attempts to derive causes from data. In one way or another, often subtle, they have confused correlation with causation. This confusion is covered up by the use of language that avoids the word "cause" and its derivatives. People often use "determine," "influence," and "predict" instead of "cause." They use "exogenous," "predetermined," and "independent" instead of "causal." They use "endogenous" and "dependent" instead of "resulting." They use "structure" instead of "causal relations."

In physics, or chemistry, or engineering, we use experiments to find out about causes. In economics, experiments are rarely done. But perhaps if we realized how little we can learn from correlations, we would do more experiments.

Correlations

In summarizing data, it is often convenient to use correlations. The variability and average level of each variable are used too, but the relations among the variables are described by the correlations. When some of the variables are not random, "correlation" is not the right word, but it still conveys the right feeling.

The long equations in many models are nothing but correlations. If we know the correlations, we can write down a large number of long equations involving different groups of variables. We can put any variable on the left-hand side, and any number of the remaining variables on the right-hand side.

For example, suppose we are interested in the adult heights of different members of a family – father, mother, son, and daughter. Assume that males and females grow to the same average height, and that children grow to the same average height as parents. Assume that the father's height and the mother's height contribute equally to a child's height, and that the heights of two children in the same family are related only through the heights of their common parents.

To figure out the correlations among all the variables, we need one more bit of information – how closely related the father's and mother's heights are. Suppose tall people tend to marry tall people, and short people tend to marry short people, so that the correlation between the height of the father and the height of the mother is 1/2. Using f, m, s, and d for the heights of the father, mother, son, and daughter, table 12.1 shows the correlation among all the variables, Note that the correlation between the son's height and the daughter's height is just as strong as the correlation between a parent's height and a child's height.

Table 12.1   Correlations of family heights

	f	m	s	d
f	1	$1/2$	$3/4$	$3/4$
m	$1/2$	1	$3/4$	$3/4$
s	$3/4$	$3/4$	1	$3/4$
d	$3/4$	$3/4$	$3/4$	1

Once we know the correlations, we can write down any equation we want for the best predictor of one variable given the values of other variables. Putting a bar over the variable we are predicting, and using h for the average adult height, we can write any of the following equations.

$$\bar{s} = \frac{1}{2}f + \frac{1}{2}m$$
$$\bar{d} = \frac{1}{2}f + \frac{1}{2}m$$
$$\bar{s} = \frac{3}{4}f + \frac{1}{4}h$$
$$\bar{d} = \frac{3}{4}m + \frac{1}{4}h$$
$$\bar{f} = \frac{3}{4}s + \frac{1}{4}h$$
$$\bar{m} = \frac{3}{4}d + \frac{1}{4}h$$
$$\bar{f} = \frac{1}{2}m + \frac{1}{2}h$$
$$\bar{m} = \frac{1}{2}f + \frac{1}{2}h$$
$$\bar{s} = \frac{3}{4}d + \frac{1}{4}h$$
$$\bar{d} = \frac{3}{4}s + \frac{1}{4}h$$
$$\bar{f} = \frac{3}{7}s + \frac{3}{7}d + \frac{1}{7}h$$
$$\bar{s} = \frac{3}{7}d + \frac{3}{7}f + \frac{1}{7}h$$
$$\bar{d} = \frac{3}{7}f + \frac{3}{7}s + \frac{1}{7}h$$
$$\bar{m} = \frac{3}{5}s + \frac{3}{5}d - \frac{2}{5}f + \frac{1}{5}h \ .$$

Any of these equations could be part of an "econometric model" of heights of parents and children. But once we know the correlations, the equations tell us nothing new. The correlations among the pairs of variables tell us everything there is to know about how the variables are statistically related. Neither these equations nor the correlations tell us much about how the variables are causally related.

Unfortunately, it's hard to interpret correlations, no matter how they are presented. When only a few variables are included in a model, it's possible that the relations we see are due to the influence of variables that are not included. But when we have a large model with many variables, there are so many relations that it becomes extremely difficult to understand them. We will look at these problems in more detail in the next section.

Causation

Econometric models are supposed to tell us about causation. Most often, they actually tell us about correlation.

Advertising and Sales

Consider the relation between advertising expenditures and sales of the advertised product. It is clear that advertising sells certain products. It is also clear that products that sell more advertise more. So the simple correlation between advertising and sales cannot be used to tell us how much an increase in advertising will increase sales in any individual case.

Firms solve this problem by looking at more than correlations. They do experiments. They advertise in some regions but not in others. They switch between print media and broadcast media. Even the experiments are of somewhat limited value, because the results can change over time or from product to product.

Furthermore, a firm that always takes what it thinks is the best approach in every market will not be able to do experiments. Then it will be very difficult to analyze the correlation between advertising and sales. One approach would be to try to include in the analysis variables other than advertising that affect sales. If we can take out the effects of these variables, perhaps we will be left with the effects of the advertising.

But this won't work, because any variable that influences future sales will also influence the level of advertising for a product. If a firm thinks a new product has great potential, for whatever reason, it will tend to spend heavily (relative to a similar product with less potential) on advertising it. It's not reasonable to expect to include all the variables that influence future sales.

If we were somehow able to measure all the variables that are related to future sales of a product, we would be able to explain the level of advertising too. We wouldn't be able to test for the independent effect of advertising, because there wouldn't be any.

When firms are acting optimally in the light of what they can know without doing experiments, we can't test the causal relation between advertising and sales. Our only hope is that firms sometimes make mistakes and thus do not act optimally.

Mistakes, such as the omission of a television commercial from its scheduled slot, can sometimes give a firm information like the information it gets from experiments. Such mistakes, though, should be identified and analyzed separately. It doesn't help to lump them in with other data on advertising and sales, as would be done with a standard econometric analysis.

It's not even clear what we would hope to show by building an econometric model of the relation between advertising and sales. That firms typically advertise to the point where an additional dollar spent on advertising generates an additional dollar in net revenue? If it doesn't tell us that, we'd better throw out the model.

Some years ago, a colleague of mine thought he had found a market where marginal revenue was greater than marginal cost. As a sideline, he went into the satin sheet business. He was really in the business of advertising satin sheets, because he didn't have to concern himself much with the production of the sheets. He placed an ad, and then as orders came in, he sent them to a "fulfillment house" that shipped the sheets.

What did he find? On average, a dollar of advertising generated a dollar of revenue, net of the costs of buying, financing, and shipping the sheets. And a dollar spent on upgrading the plate used in printing the ads generated a dollar of extra revenue net of costs. The firms already in the satin sheet business had made the market very efficient.

This suggests a different approach to the problem of building a model of the relation between advertising and sales. We might develop a theory of advertising based on the idea that firms almost always act rationally in deciding where and how to advertise and how much to spend on advertising. We might introduce a variety of factors that affect the nature of a firm's advertising. If we are ambitious, we may even use the notion that consumers respond rationally to advertising as a source of product information.

Using this theory, we can take the amount and type of advertising actually done as optimal, and relate it to the type of product advertised and other factors. We won't need to use figures on future sales at all, but we will include past sales of the product, and past sales of related products, as factors affecting the current level of advertising.

The result will be a model of factors that seem to affect advertising, rather than a model of the relation between advertising and sales. We will estimate correlations, and fit the theory of how various factors affect optimal advertising to the numbers we find. The correlations will not tell us directly about the causal relation between the factors we look at and the firm's advertising.

Money and Economic Activity

For a second example, consider the relation between money and economic activity. When economic activity grows faster than usual, the money stock tends to grow faster than usual, and when the money stock grows faster than usual, economic activity tends to grow faster than usual. Slower than usual growth in the money stock tends to be associated with slower than usual growth in economic activity too. In other words, growth in the money stock and growth in economic activity are correlated.

How are we to interpret this correlation? Many economists believe that Federal Reserve open market operations affect economic activity. I believe that the level of economic activity affects the demand for money, which affects the stock of money, but that open market operations do not affect the level of economic activity. In my theory, the money supply function and the money demand function are identical. Whenever the demand for money changes, the money stock changes to accommodate the change in demand without any significant influence or interference by the Federal Reserve Board.[6]

The correlation does not tell us the direction of causation. In the Great Depression, income and money both fell sharply. But did the fall in the money stock cause the fall in income? Or did the fall in income cause the fall in the money stock?

Leads and lags in the relation between two variables can give some information about the direction of causation, but even this information is hard to interpret. We are tempted to say that if changes in money tend to lead changes in income, the causal chain runs from money to income. But this conclusion is not warranted.

The problem is that there may be a third factor causing changes in both money and income. It may act on money more quickly than it acts on income. Wealth, as measured by the level of stock prices, acts this way.

In fact, we find that changes in stock prices neither lead nor lag changes in money, while they lead changes in income.[7] If demand for money is related to wealth, we would expect changes in stock prices and changes in money to be related with little or no lag. If stock prices reflect anticipated corporate profits and thus anticipated economic conditions, we would expect changes in stock prices and changes in income to be related with a lag. Thus the lag between changes in money and changes in income may be due to the common influence of changes in wealth.

We just can't use correlations, with or without leads and lags, to determine causation. We could use experiments with Federal Reserve policy to find out whether money affects income, but experiments like that have not been considered acceptable.

If we're not going to do experiments, then we are forced to test a theory of the relation between money and income by whether it is consistent with the observed correlations (as both theories mentioned above are) and by whether it seems plausible.

A plausible theory is one whose assumptions seem reasonable, or one whose predictions would not change much if its assumptions were replaced by more reasonable assumptions. A plausible theory is one that does not imply consistent, easy to exploit profit opportunities. A plausible theory is one that fits both everyday experience and correlations that come out of statistical analysis.

There just isn't any easy way to test a theory, or to show the direction of causation between two variables. There will often be several plausible theories consistent with the observed correlations. If we can't do experiments, all we can do is to keep making our theories more plausible, and to keep testing the theories against measured correlations. Constructing an econometric model is just a way of testing a theory against measured correlations.

Consumption and Output

Consumption and output show a positive correlation. Unusual increases or decreases in consumption are associated with unusual increases or decreases in output. But what does this mean?

Some theories assign a causal role to consumption. People cut their consumption, which reduces business for many firms, which reduces output, which reduces income, which may cause people to cut their consumption even more.

Other theories assign a more passive role to consumption. People cut their consumption when wealth falls and when they expect output to fall. If output does not fall, the cut in consumption will mean higher savings.[8]

There is no easy way to use correlations to distinguish between these two theories. We can construct models of each that will be consistent with observed correlations between consumption and output. We shouldn't take any one model seriously just because it can be made to fit the data.

I have been unable to think of any way to distinguish between the various possible econometric models involving consumption and output – at least any way that involves standard methods for constructing econometric models.

Supply and Demand

Econometric models are often developed to relate the supply and demand for a single commodity or group of commodities. We may set supply, which depends on price and other variables, equal to demand, which also depends on price and other variables. When supply and demand are equal, let's call their common value Q. Let's write P for the price of the commodity.

The basic correlation in a model of supply and demand is the correlation between P and Q. Unfortunately, this can't tell us much about either supply or demand. Changes in demand will make P and Q move in the same direction, and will tell us about supply, if supply doesn't change. Changes in supply will make P and Q move in opposite directions, and will tell us about demand, if demand doesn't change.

But what happens is that both supply and demand are continuously changing, so the correlation between P and Q doesn't tell a clear story about either one. We can try bringing in other variables, but most other variables are related to both supply and demand, or to neither supply nor demand, so we can't use correlations between P and the other variables or correlations between Q and the other variables to tell us about supply alone or about demand alone.

Demand for Gasoline

When the price of gasoline goes up, how much will consumption of gasoline fall in the short run? How much will it fall in the long run? How does the change in consumption depend on the source of the price increase?

It's very hard to use observations about the price of gasoline and the amount consumed to answer these questions. Because some price changes are caused by demand changes, a price increase will often be associated with an increase in consumption, rather than with a decrease, or with a relatively small decrease in consumption.

What about looking at variations across states in the price of gasoline and in the amount consumed per person? The problem here is that there are so many other variables, related to both price and consumption, that it will be very, very difficult to hold other things the same. Population density for example, should be negatively related to price because of economies of scale, but should be negatively related to amount consumed per person because people who live in apartments don't use as much gasoline as people who live on ranches.

Even the increases in price that are often attributed to collusion among the petroleum-exporting countries may be partly due to increases in demand. Increases in demand for a product that theoretically has a fixed total supply will increase the price that a cartel will charge, just as they would increase the price that competitive producers charge. Thus we can't use the consumption changes associated with such price increases as direct evidence on the sensitivity of consumption to price.

Taxes and Work

We tax high incomes at high rates, and subsidize low incomes through programs such as public housing, food stamps, unemployment compensation, social security, subsidized public transport, and welfare. Theory suggests that high-income people may work a lot in spite of high tax rates, but that low-income people may respond strongly to payments they receive only if they don't work.

How can we estimate the strength of this incentive effect? We want to know, in effect, how a change in a person's wage will affect the number of hours he puts in. Even if we can observe hours worked and after-tax wages, it will be very difficult to estimate the strength of the effect.

Estimating the sensitivity of work to wages is difficult for reasons very much like those that make estimating the sensitivity of gasoline consumption to gasoline prices difficult. If wages go up because work becomes more difficult or leisure becomes more attractive, then work may go down rather than up. If worsening economic conditions cause the government to increase its subsidies to non-workers, it will be hard to tell whether the decline in work is due to the subsidies or to the worsening economic conditions.

Similarly, variations in tax rates and variations in hours worked across states cannot be used in any obvious way to tell how sensitive hours worked are to after-tax wages. Tax rates do not vary randomly. Presumably they vary mostly because of differences between the states. These differences will also be related to hours worked. For example, taxes in some states may be high because people in those states care more about the poor, hence are willing to work hard to pay the taxes to provide services for the poor. How can we separate the effects of taxes from the effects of these other variables?

Even if we have an econometric model with many variables and many equations, we will mostly be estimating correlations. Correlations won't tell us much about either the demand for gasoline or the supply of work.

Forecasting

It is easier to use correlations for forecasting than it is to interpret them. If we're using them for forecasting, we don't have to understand them. Thus it is easier to use econometric models for forecasting than it is to interpret the coefficients. Understanding a model helps only in that it may give us confidence that the coefficients will be stable through time.

Changes in stock prices are correlated with future changes in corporate earnings, hence with future changes in GNP. Since stock prices reflect expectations about future cash flows, we can have confidence that this relation will persist.

Changes in interest rates seem to be correlated with future changes in GNP too. Since we don't understand why this correlation exists, we will watch closely for signs that it has shifted. But so long as it persists, it can be used in forecasting GNP.

Even the best forecasts may not be very good. The forward exchange rate between two currencies will be the best forecast of the future spot rate, for certain purposes, if the forward market is efficient. The correlation between the forward rate and the future spot rate may be low, but the model that says the forward rate is the expected future spot rate is the best there is. There's no reason to add any other variables or to construct an elaborate econometric model using those variables.[9]

Forecasts based on efficient markets can sometimes be very useful. For example, the futures market for gold usually indicates that the price of gold is expected to rise at about the current interest rate. Since returns on gold are largely independent of returns on securities, that means that gold is a natural part of most individual portfolios. Holdings of gold are not taxed unless gains are realized, so gold has a high after-tax expected return for an asset whose risk can be diversified away.

As the gold example indicates, a good forecasting model need not be complex. When we make use of the information in efficient markets, the model may contain only one variable, or at most just a few variables.

Errors

One of the problems with econometric models is that all the variables are observed with error. We estimate correlations between the variables we observe, while we might like to know the correlations between the unobservable variables without errors. What's more, the correlations are often unstable, so our estimates for one period may not be valid for a later period.

These problems should make us very cautious about using econometric models for forecasting, because we learn to forecast observed variables, and we want forecasts of the unobserved variables. They should make us even more cautious about interpreting the correlations or coefficients in an econometric model, because the correlation between two observed variables can be very different from the correlation between the corresponding unobserved variables.

For a simple example, let's look at the relation between inflation and exchange rates. The simplest theory relating these variables is called purchasing power parity. It says that when the inflation rate in one country is higher than it might have been, holding real variables and other countries' inflation rates constant, that country's exchange rate will depreciate more than it might have depreciated or will appreciate less than it might have appreciated.

Purchasing power parity theory does not have a causal structure; it merely predicts certain correlations. Under fixed exchange rates, a country may increase its inflation rate by devaluing its currency. Under floating exchange rates, higher inflation in one country than in other countries may cause the value of its currency to decline.

To test purchasing power parity, we can look at correlations among inflation rates, changes in exchange rates and such real variables as tariffs and exchange controls that should affect both exchange rates and inflation. At first glance, these correlations often seem inconsistent with purchasing power parity. Changes in exchange rates may be far from differences between inflation rates.

One reason for that is that the real variables are not being held constant. An important reason, though, is that the theory deals, not with actual inflation rates, but with differences between actual inflation rates and inflation rates that might have been. We can't observe the inflation rates that might have been. Thus it's hard to reject purchasing power parity based on correlations between observable variables. The difference between the observable inflation rates and the unobservable variables we would like to use is just too great.

If we accept purchasing power parity, then changes in the value of the dollar do not cause changes in trade patterns. Changes in the relative prices of imports and exports may show up, though, partly as changes in the value of the dollar. Nominal values may be symptoms, but not causes, of what's happening in the real international economy.

Since this theory is so simple, and has such interesting policy implications, it would be nice to know whether it's true or not. Unfortunately, correlations between observable variables won't tell us, at least not without a lot of other evidence.

Solutions

What are some possible solutions to the problems of trying to find causal relations in observational data?

I have not been able to think of any general solutions to the problem. It is possible that the methods used must depend on the special facts of each case. For example, it may be that close attention to the effects of "accidents" will give us information that we could not get by looking at the normal operations of a market or the economy. Accidents that are truly random, though, are rare.

I have studied the relation between stock price changes and stock price volatility changes.[10] The possible causal relations included direct causation (from price changes to volatility changes), reverse causation (from volatility changes to price changes), and causation from changes in other underlying factors. I interpreted the magnitude of the relation I found as suggesting that at least two of these kinds of causation must be operating. I proposed a direct test for reverse causation, but the test did not give conclusive results.

I'm not sure how to generalize these methods, though. Both seemed specific to the facts of this problem. For example, the test for reverse causation depended on the notion that changes in expectations of future volatility should be reflected immediately in stock prices. With economic data other than stock prices, this test might have no analogue.

There is hope. We can do more experiments, when the answers we seek are worth enough to justify the cost of experimenting. We can look for problem-specific ways to identify cause and effect.[11] I doubt, however, that traditional econometric methods will survive.

Glossary
The Language of Econometrics

The trouble with econometric models is that they encourage us to read correlations as indicating causation. We can see this by looking more closely at the language of econometrics.

An *exogenous variable* is supposed to be a causal variable, if the structure of a model has economic meaning. In fact, it is usually just a variable that is put on the right-hand side of equations in a model, but not on the left-hand side.

Similarly, an *endogenous variable* is supposed to be a caused variable. In fact, it is usually just a variable that shows up at least once on the left-hand side of an equation.

A *reduced form model* is supposed to show all the direct and indirect effects of the exogenous variables on the endogenous variables. Usually, though, it is simply a statement of correlation between the left- and right-hand side variables.

A *structural model* is supposed to show the causal relations among the variables in the model. That's why some variables in a structural model usually appear on the left-hand side of one equation and the right-hand side of the others – to show a causal chain. Most often, a structural model cannot be interpreted causally. Regressions alone cannot tell about the strength of causal relations. A structural model usually tells about statistical structure, but not about economic structure.

A model is *misspecified* when it does not reflect the causal relations among the variables. Some forms of misspecification make sense only under a causal interpretation. For example, *omitted variables* can't be a problem if you're only interested in correlation. A sensible regression can be done (when the variables are joint normal) for any choice of right-hand side variables. Similarly, the residuals in a regression among joint normal variables can't be correlated with the independent variables, if all the coefficients are chosen to minimize the sum of squared errors. Less commonly, a model is "misspecified" when it does not correctly reflect the statistical relations among the variables, so it is not the best possible model for prediction.

The *identification problem* is a way of describing the inability to make causal inferences from the coefficients of estimated equations. The phrase is especially used in connection with the inability to derive demand curves or supply curves from observations on price and quantity. Unfortunately, this problem is very difficult to solve. The standard method that is tried involves searching for a variable that is related to demand but not to supply, or to supply but not to demand. Do such variables exist?

A model has *errors in variables* when the observed variables differ from the variables we would like to observe. Every model has this problem. It means the estimated correlations will differ from the correlations we would like to estimate between unobserved variables.

The *multicollinearity problem* is serious when you are trying to assess causal ties. When two variables are closely related, a correlation between one variable and a third might reflect a causal connection between the second and third variables. If you are only interested in statistical structure, the only problem caused by multicollinearity is that when both variables are used on the right-hand side of an equation, the coefficients of these two variables will be estimated with considerable error. Equations can also be estimated with only one of the collinear variables at a time; the coefficients will not be the same as when both are used, but in a statistical model, there is no reason why they should be the same.

An *instrumental variable* is supposed to help in assessing causality. When two variables clearly have common causes, the correlation between them can be very hard to interpret. If we replace one of them with an instrument, we hope that the causal relations will be more nearly from one variable to the other. Unfortunately, it's hard to find instruments like this. Thus it's hard to put a causal interpretation on correlations involving instrumental variables.

I would like to thank Michael Jensen, Merton Miller, Robert Pindyck, David Ranson, Harvey Rosen, Julio Rotemberg, and Lawrence Summers for comments (often critical) on earlier drafts of this chapter.

Notes

1 Pratt and Schlaifer (1981) discuss this problem too. Their abstract starts as follows: "We inquire into the conditions under which nonexperimental data reveal effects of a kind revealed by randomized experiments and relevant to decisions, although we define effects without regard to either. We argue that the general linear model as usually presented by statisticians fails to distinguish between effects and regression coefficients."
2 The econometric texts I have found most helpful are Christ (1966); Malinvaud (1966); Hanushek and Jackson (1977); and Leamer (1978).

3 There is a literature within econometrics that aims to test for causation in a narrower sense. See, for example, Sims (1972, pp. 540–52). For a critical review of this literature, and a technical definition of causality, see Granger (1980, pp. 329–52).

4 See Black, Jensen, and Scholes (1972, pp. 79–121); Black and Scholes (1974, pp. 1–22); and Black (1976, pp. 177–81).

5 Leamer (1978) writes in part about what people do when they search for the econometric model that best fits the data. This can mean searching for causes, or searching for the best statistical model for the data. He emphasizes the search for the best statistical model. Sargent (1981, pp. 213–48) outlines some of what must be done to derive causal implications correctly.

6 My theory is described in chapter 2.

7 Rozeff (1974, pp. 245–303) and Rogalsky and Vinso (1977, pp. 1017–30) study the relation between money and stock prices. Sims (1972) studies the relations between money and income.

8 For an analysis of both kinds of theory, see Sargent (1979).

9 Cornell (1977, pp. 55–65) analyzes the relation between forward and spot exchange rates. If you are trying to create a forecast with the smallest possible average error, the forward rate may not be the best forecast of the spot rate. You may want to put in estimated risk premiums. For any other purpose, it probably pays to use the forward rate as if it were the expected spot rate, even though it isn't. See also Black (1981).

10 Black (1976).

11 Pratt and Schlaifer (1981) suggest "thinking hard about unobserved variables that may have affected observed variables," among other things.

References

Black, Fischer 1976: Studies of stock price volatility changes. *Proceedings of the 1976 Meetings of the American Statistical Association, Business and Economics Statistics Section*, 177–81.

Black, Fischer 1981: A simple discounting rule. Memorandum.

Black, Fischer and Scholes, Myron 1974: The effects of dividend yield and dividend policy on common stock prices and returns. *Journal of Financial Economics*, May, 1–22.

Black, Fischer, Jensen, Michael C. and Scholes, Myron 1972: The capital asset pricing model: some empirical tests. In Michael C. Jensen (ed.), *Studies in the Theory of Capital Markets*. New York: Praeger, 79–121.

Christ, Carl F. 1966: *Econometric Models and Methods*. New York: Wiley.

Cornell, Bradford 1977: Spot rates and exchange market efficiency. *Journal of Financial Economics*, August, 55–65.

Granger, C. W. J. 1980: Testing for causality: a personal viewpoint. *Journal of Economic Dynamics and Control*, November, 329–52.

Hanushek, Eric A. and Jackson, John E. 1977: *Statistical Methods for Social Scientists*. New York: Academic Press.

Leamer, Edward E. 1978: *Specification Searches*. New York: Wiley.

Malinvaud, E. 1966: *Statistical Methods of Econometrics* (Mrs. A. Silvey, trans.). Amsterdam: North-Holland.

Pratt, John W. and Schlaifer, Robert 1981: On the nature and discovery of structure. Unpublished memorandum.

Rogalsky, Richard J. and Vinso, Joseph D. 1977: Stock returns, money supply, and the direction of causality. *Journal of Finance*, September, 1017–30.

Rozeff, Michael S. 1974: Money and stock prices: market efficiency and the lag in effect of monetary policy. *Journal of Financial Economics*, September, 245–303.

Sargent, Thomas J. 1979: *Macroeconomic Theory*. New York: Academic Press.

Sargent, Thomas J. 1981: Interpreting economic time series. *Journal of Political Economy*, April, 213–48.

Sims, Christopher A. 1972: Money, income, and causality. *American Economic Review*, September, 540–52.

13

General Equilibrium and Business Cycles

The general equilibrium models in this paper, with complete markets, can give the major features of business cycles. The models include real investment, but information is costless and is available to everyone at the same time. Fluctuations in the match between resources and wants across many sectors create major fluctuations in output and unemployment, because moving resources from one sector to another is costly. Fluctuations in the demand for the services of durable goods causes much larger fluctuations in the output of durables, and causes unemployment that takes the form of temporary layoffs. Since specialized factors cooperate in producing goods and services, it makes sense to lay people off in groups rather than lowering wages and waiting for them to quit. Similarly, a vacancy is created when a specialized factor is missing from such a group. Technology comes with varying levels of risk and expected return associated with the degree of specialization. More specialization means more severe fluctuations and a higher average level of unemployment, along with a higher average level of output and growth. Monetary policy, interest rates, and fiscal policy have no special roles to play in the model.

Introduction

Business cycles are fluctuations in economic activity. Most measures of economic activity look something like a random walk with drift: successive changes in the level of economic activity are largely independent.[1] Changes in the level of economic activity in different sectors are quite highly correlated, but output of durables fluctuates more than output of non-durables. Output of durables and unemployment both show some tendency to return, over time, to normal levels. The normal levels of durables output and unemployment tend to change, so the path of any measure of economic activity can be quite complex. We will take unemployment as the variable that best captures the fluctuations we want to understand.[2]

General equilibrium models[3] take individuals as maximizing the expected value of a utility function, where utility depends on consumption at various times of various goods and services, and on state variables that can be taken to represent tastes.[4] We will assume that markets are complete, so we can show that one does not need incomplete markets to understand the major features of business cycles: this means that the state variables representing tastes are observable, and are the basis for some of the traded securities.[5] We will include physical investment: in fact, we will assume that a variety of technologies are available at any time. The available technologies also depend on state variables. Individuals bear costs in shifting their human capital from one sector to another, and in shifting physical capital from one sector to another. These adjustment costs seem largely internal: I do not believe that significant externalities in this process have been clearly identified.[6]

Thus the models in this chapter are entirely consistent with maximizing behavior on the part of individuals and firms in light of the information they have had and the opportunities they face.[7] It hardly makes sense, in my view, to work with models that do not assume maximizing behavior. At the same time, there is no easy way to test these models or to estimate the constants in a model.[8] The models I discuss are very incomplete, and it is always very difficult to use observations of economic data to help us understand the economy. Since we do not know the true model, correlation implies almost nothing about causation.

A Multisector Model

It is possible to model business cycles using a model with a single good and a single composite production sector.[9] Fluctuations in economic activity in a model like this appear as fluctuations in the stock of capital.[10] Such a model, however, does not lend itself to an analysis of unemployment. To have unemployment in a model with maximizing behavior, we need a multisector model.[11]

Both human and physical capital will be specialized, because specialization increases expected productivity. However, there are shocks to both tastes and technology in the form of unexpected shifts in the state variables in the economy. As a result, we find ourselves with a capital stock whose composition is different from the composition we would have chosen had we known in advance what the world would be like. The match between resources and wants is not perfect.

We will want to shift capital from the sectors where we have too much to the sectors where we have too little. Relative prices will motivate this shift. But the less advance notice we have, the more costly it is to shift capital between sectors.[12] Also, the more different the sectors are from one another, the more costly it is to shift capital from one to the other.

Shocks that create a poor match, which will mean large shifts of human capital between sectors, cause unemployment and a decline in output. Shocks that create a good match will bring unemployment below its average level and output above its average level. As resources are shifted between sectors, the match will improve. The shocks combined with the shift of resources will cause unemployment to wander around its average level: when it is near its average level, its movements will be largely random; but when it is far from its average level, the random movements will be combined with a drift back toward its average level. Of course, the average level will also be changing through time as tastes and technology change.

Shifting resources between sectors is just one source of unemployment. Other sources will have somewhat different behavior. Also, a shift of resources can occur without unemployment. Job changes can occur without an intervening period of search or waiting for a new job. This model suggests, though, that job turnover associated with a change from one employer to another will be higher in bad times than in good times.

The more sectors there are, the more ways there are for the match to go wrong. A model that has only consumption goods and investment goods will not be able to generate much unemployment through this device. A model with a single good will not produce any of this kind of unemployment at all.

Similarly, no one source of uncertainty, such as uncertainty about relative prices associated with price level uncertainty, will generate much unemployment in this model. It is the large number of partly independent shocks to different sectors that generates significant unemployment.

Unemployment generated this way will show considerable persistence, because it costs less to move resources between sectors slowly than to move them quickly. A mismatch between resources and wants will be corrected at a rate that balances the benefits of a better match against the costs of a faster movement of resources.

The government can reduce the unemployment rate by subsidizing declining sectors and taxing rising sectors, or by ordering the goods and services produced in the declining sectors. This will improve welfare only if one person's unemployment imposes unavoidable costs on others. The case for the existence of this kind of externality has not been made, in my view.[13]

To make this model more concrete, let's use a simple example with just two sectors. Imagine that all individuals are identical, and the world lasts for only one period. At the start of the period, an individual chooses amounts x and y of resources 1 and 2 from a constant elasticity of transformation production frontier:[14]

$$1 = (x^b/c + y^b/d)^{1/b} \qquad \begin{matrix} b > 1 \\ c > 0 \\ d > 0. \end{matrix} \qquad (13.1)$$

The individual chooses x and y knowing that his utility function will be Cobb–Douglas, of the form

$$u = x^a y^{1-a} \qquad (13.2)$$

but without knowing the exact value of a.

At the end of the period, the individual learns the value of a, and has a chance to transform x into y or y into x. The terms on which the transformation can be made take the form of another constant elasticity of transformation production frontier that is tangent to the first frontier at the point x, y. The second frontier is inside the first frontier because last-minute changes are more costly than changes made in advance.

$$1 = (x^{b^*}/c^* + y^{b^*}/d^*)^{1/b^*} \qquad \begin{matrix} b^* > b \\ c^* > 0 \\ d^* > 0. \end{matrix} \qquad (13.3)$$

The final amounts chosen, x^* and y^*, are determined by the point at which the new production frontier (13.3) is tangent to the indifference curves (13.2). It turns out that this point can be derived analytically with no trouble. First, the values of b^*, c^*, and d^* are determined by:

$$1 = x^{b^*}/c^* + y^{b^*}/d^*, \qquad (13.4)$$

$$x^{b^*}/c^* = x^b/c, \qquad (13.5)$$

$$y^{b^*}/d^* = y^b/d. \qquad (13.6)$$

Then the values of x^* and y^* are determined by:

$$x^{*b^*}/c^* = a,$$ (13.7)

$$y^{*b^*}/d^* = 1 - a.$$ (13.8)

A perfect match occurs when x^* is equal to x and y^* is equal to y. In that case, it would not have helped to know a in advance. That represents the maximum possible utility for the individual. The worse the match, the lower the individual's utility will be.

A Durable Goods Model

In addition to the process involving a match between resources and wants across sectors, there is a process operating within any sector that produces durable goods. This process helps explain both temporary layoffs and the exact form that the business cycle takes.[15]

Suppose that demand falls for the services of durable goods produced by a given sector. Since the stock of durable goods deteriorates slowly, output of these goods will fall sharply until the stock of goods comes more into line with demand, given the cost of producing new goods. The decline in output will be associated with a fall in the relative price of these goods.[16]

As the stock of durables comes into line, output will gradually rise, unless changed by a new shock to tastes or technology. Thus durables will introduce a pattern of a sharp fall in output followed by a gradual rise, or a sharp rise in output followed by a gradual fall. These patterns will be added to a pattern of random changes due to new shocks, so they will not be seen in pure form.

Output of durables will respond more to new information than output of non-durables. Thus sectors producing durables should show larger cyclical fluctuations than sectors producing non-durables.

Moreover, some of the changes in output in a durable goods sector will be temporary. A temporary decline in output will be associated with temporary layoffs. Thus the behavior of durable goods helps us understand another component of unemployment.[17]

Again, let's make the discussion more concrete by working out a simple example. Assume that the loss of utility from having the wrong stock of durables is proportional to the square of the difference between the actual stock x and the target stock k, and has weight g^2. Assume that the loss of utility associated with adjusting the stock of durables is proportional to the square of the rate of adjustment $\dot{x}$. Assume that we can ignore discounting. Finally, assume that output y is for replacement of depreciated capital at rate qx plus adjustment of the stock of capital at rate $\dot{x}$.

Assume all individuals are identical, and want to minimize the total loss of utility over an infinite lifetime associated with a shock that moves k away from the initial value x^* of the stock x of durables.

$$\text{Minimize:} \int_0^\infty [g^2(x-k)^2 + \dot{x}^2]\,dt. \tag{13.9}$$

The individual chooses a path for $\dot{x}$ that minimizes the value of this integral. Using the calculus of variations, we find that the solution is:

$$x - k = (x^* - k)e^{-gt}, \tag{13.10}$$

$$\dot{x} = -g(x^* - k)e^{-gt}, \tag{13.11}$$

$$y = qx - g(x^* - k)e^{-gt}. \tag{13.12}$$

We can see that a sudden change in k will cause a sudden change in y, followed by a gradual change in y in the opposite direction.

Unemployment

Unemployment, in the models outlined above, takes two forms. One form is associated with costly shifts of human capital between sectors when there is a poor match between resources and wants. The other is associated with temporary layoffs when times are bad in durable goods sectors. These two kinds of unemployment will tend to rise and fall together, though they will not always be perfectly in phase. Output will tend to fall when unemployment rises, and to rise when unemployment falls. Unemployment will be countercyclical; or if we use unemployment to define the business cycle, we can say that output is procyclical.[18]

So far, the models have nothing to say about why firms fire or lay off their employees in bad times rather than lowering wages so that the desired number will quit. Some of the reasons are obvious. An employee who quits will not generally be eligible for unemployment benefits under current law, so the employee and employer may agree to make it an involuntary termination. An employee who has been notified through a wage reduction that it's time to think about leaving may not be very productive: he may even do things that harm his employer.

More generally, though, I think the reason lies in the fact that production involves the cooperation of a number of people with specialized skills. A firm cares about more than just the number of employees. When a few key employees leave, the others may become much less productive. Thus it is natural to close down a whole unit at once, and to lay off or transfer essentially all the employees of that unit.

The cooperative production notion may also help us understand vacancies. When a key person has left a unit that is being kept open, or when a key person is missing from a unit being reopened, it can be important to find a replacement for that person quickly. A firm will use advertising or hiring bonuses to do it. It will not use high wages for that person unless a person with the desired skills will receive high wages anywhere he works.

Can the models outlined above help us understand why workers with less seniority are generally laid off first, or why young people have a relatively high unemployment rate? I think so. Young people have more time to recoup the costs of changing sectors, so they will favor an arrangement that gives them higher pay than they would otherwise get in exchange for the risk of being laid off first in a downturn. A worker with less seniority has fewer skills specific to the job, so a relatively small decline in the sector the worker is in will make other jobs more attractive.

These models do imply that in a downturn, the rate at which workers move from one sector to another will rise. This may be hard to see at first, since people who are laid off may not know yet whether they will be changing sectors or not. The number of quits may fall in a downturn, because of a reduction in the number of vacancies (as defined above) and because people who would otherwise quit may now be laid off. This will be especially true in sectors producing durable goods.

Since we are assuming that markets are complete, long-term contracts do not play any special role.[19] It is not restrictive to have long-term contracts available along with shorter term contracts.

Choice among Technologies

In the models outlined above, we discussed the choice among technologies only in very general terms. An individual could choose a point along a production frontier that put resources into each of two sectors. Sectors, however, can be defined in many ways. A more specialized worker and a less specialized worker can be taken as being in different sectors, even though they participate in production processes with the same outputs.

Specialization is associated with both risk and productivity. When certain factors affecting tastes and technology are uncertain, there is a risk that a specialized factor will not be wanted. On the other hand, if it is wanted, the productivity of a specialized factor will generally be higher than the productivity of a non-specialized factor doing the same job. In other words, greater specialization means that when the match between resources and wants is good, output will be very high, but when the match is bad, output will be very low. It is very costly to move a specialized factor from one kind of task to another.

Note that the risks in the use of specialized resources do not cancel. High demand in one sector does not offset low demand in another, since it is costly to shift resources from the low-demand sector to the high-demand sector. When the match is poor, output will be low and unemployment will be high.

Individuals will choose investments in human and physical capital that reflect their preferences. The more tolerant of risk they are, and the more tolerant of unemployment they are, the more specialized the chosen resources will be. Higher risk and higher unemployment will be associated with higher expected output and growth.

Note that if markets are incomplete, people will be less able to exchange risks, so they will choose less specialization, less severe business cycles, lower output, and lower growth. Similarly, if people have less information, a given degree of specialization will be riskier, so they will cut back both risk and expected productivity.

Note also that the magnitude of fluctuations in output and unemployment tells us very little about welfare. Since large fluctuations are associated with rapid growth, there is no index of welfare that takes into account only the magnitude of fluctuations. The government can dampen fluctuations by taxing risk or by taxing specialization in any of several ways, but this seems more likely to reduce welfare than to increase it, because it introduces unnecessary distortions.

Other Matters

In a model with complete markets, inflation will play no role at all. In the real world, inflation is associated with certain costs, such as the cost of changing prices, the cost of contracting in real terms, and the cost of economizing on the use of currency. With one exception, these costs seem small compared to the cost of a mismatch between resources and wants.

The exception is that when inflation turns to large deflation and the nominal riskless short-term interest rate falls to zero, we have a "currency trap." The real interest rate is forced to be higher than it would be in the absence of currency. This can cause major dislocations, and I believe it was one reason for the severity of the Great Depression.

I believe that monetary policy is not a cause of variations in the rate of inflation.[20] Even if it does influence inflation, though, it will not have a significant influence on business cycles under the models outlined above.

Similarly, fiscal policy can affect the business cycle in ways discussed above. The government can subsidize declining sectors or buy their output. It can tax specialization or risk-taking. It will thereby reduce the magnitude of fluctuations and the average level of unemployment, but will probably reduce welfare at the same time because it will distort investment choice. Similarly it can subsidize unemployment by paying generous unemployment benefits.[21] Assuming that these activities are limited, fiscal policy will not play a significant role in either increasing or decreasing the magnitude of business cycles.

Notes

1 Nelson and Plosser (1981) discuss the random walk nature of macroeconomic time series.

2 This characterization of business cycles is close to Arrow's (1978, p. 160). For more extensive characterizations of business cycles that are consistent with general equilibrium models, see Lucas (1977, p. 9), Kydland and Prescott (1978, pp. 1–2), and Hodrick and Prescott (1981).

3 For analyses of general equilibrium models, see Arrow (1971), Debreu (1959), and Hirshleifer (1970).

4 The utility functions used in general equilibrium models are often assumed to be state-independent. For example, Diamond (1967) uses a state-independent utility function. He notes (p. 761, n. 6) that this is a restrictive assumption. Hirshleifer (1970, p. 220) uses a "uniqueness" axiom to rule out state-dependent utility functions. Phelps (1962, 1967, p. 141) uses a utility function that is independent of both time and state. On the other hand, Fama (1970) and Feiger (1976) use models with state-dependent

utility functions. The original von Neumann–Morgenstern (1953) axioms ensure the existence of utility functions defined over both states and consumption streams, but Marshak (1950, p. 113) eliminates the state dependence in his version of the existence theorem. Lucas (1977, pp. 20, 25) includes changing tastes as part of his theory of business cycles. Krelle (1973, esp. pp. 105–6 and pp.115–16) discusses several ways in which tastes change, involving the influence of past consumption of a good on its present and future utility. Vickrey (1964, pp. 23–4) describes, without bringing them into his later theories, various kinds of changes in tastes that may be important in the behavior of an economy. He mentions in particular the conscious development of tastes, either by the individual or by others.

5 The use of state-dependent utility functions does not imply that taste changes are being used as a catch-all explanation for anything that cannot otherwise be explained since tastes are taken to be observable. I will assume that the utility function itself is constant: at that level, tastes are constant too. Stigler (1966, p. 39) argues that it is best to treat tastes as fixed at a lower level: that it is best to use a state-dependent utility function, in effect. Stigler and Becker (1977, p. 76) say: "The establishment of the proposition that one may usefully treat tastes as stable over time and similar among people is the central task of this essay." But in the examples they give, it is more the highest level utility function that is constant. They redefine commodities in a way that effectively indexes them by the state of the world. The use of state-indexed commodities as arguments in the utility function is equivalent to the use of a state-dependent utility function. Pollack (1978, p. 375) notes that Stigler and Becker should be objecting to the use of unobservables, whether of tastes or technology, rather than to the use of taste differences and taste change.

6 The use of adjustment costs in production functions has been formalized by Lucas (1967), Uzawa (1969), and Jorgenson (1972). The idea that there are adjustment costs in shifting labor from one sector to another has been developed by Herberg (1972). This model has been extended to allow for finite adjustment costs for both labor and capital by Herberg and Kemp (1972).

7 Lucas (1975, pp. 1113–14) gives a compelling argument for using models based on maximizing behavior. The trouble with models containing disequilibrium or abitrary elements is that they are as unstable as the economy itself is. The arbitrary elements surely change, but the ways in which they change are not specified in the model. And it is usually true that if all economic agents come to have a full understanding of a disequilibrium model, the model will no longer describe the world correctly. Models based on the work of Keynes (1936, 1965) have such disequilibrium elements as an interest rate that differs from the marginal product of capital, or a wage that is not free to move. Models based on the work of Lucas (1975) depend on easily cured ignorance about the current state of the world and on inability to create simple securities.

8 The difficulties with the use of econometrics in trying to discover the structure of the economy are discussed in chapter 12, and also in Pratt and Schlaifer (1982), and Leamer (1982).

9 Merton's (1973) intertemporal capital pricing model can be used as a model of business cycles, though he doesn't suggest such a use.

10 Kydland and Prescott (1978, pp. 3–4) argue plausibly that we can characterize the elements responsible for the persistence of business cycles as "capital-like elements." Their discussion (p. 1) of business cycles has at least two other features in common with the model in this chapter: the notion that taste changes are important, and the notion that the effects of certain kinds of shocks cannot be diversified away.

11 Lucas and Prescott (1974, p. 190) set up a multisector model of unemployment with stochastic demand in each market. They impose constraints on the model that keep it from being a model of business cycles. Hayek (1939) includes as part of his theory the notion that specialization of labor in the presence of uncertainty is one cause of fluctuations in employment. Kydland (1980) has a real business cycle model in which costs of adjustment between sectors are important.

12 Alchian (1959) discusses the relation between production cost and such factors as the amount of time available for planning the production run.

13 Diamond (1981) discusses some possible external effects of this kind.

14 Powell and Gruen (1968) discuss this kind of production frontier.

15 The role played by intermediate goods in Long and Plosser (1982) is similar to the role played in this model by durable goods. Kydland and Prescott's (1981) "time to build" also involves the effects of durable goods. Sargent (1979, pp. 160–70) has an equilibrium theory of layoffs in which "sticky" wages play a role.

16 This kind of argument is standard in accelerator models. For a traditional discussion of the accelerator in business cycle theory, see Hicks (1946, esp. pp. 299–302). Lucas (1977, p. 23) has a more modern description. Durable goods also play an important role in Kydland and Prescott's (1980) "competitive theory of fluctuations."

17 In particular, it is not necessary to assume non-separable utility. Barro and King (1982) discuss the differences between models with separable and non-separable utility. Durable goods play an important role in their models, too.

18 In Long and Plosser (1982), unemployment will tend to rise when output rises if producers switch inputs more easily than consumers switch between consumption of the commodity and consumption of leisure.

19 For models in which long-term contracts do play a special role, see Burdett and Mortensen (1980).

20 For an introduction to my views on monetary policy, see chapter 2. For an alternate view of monetary policy in a real business cycle model, see King and Plosser (1982).

21 Benjamin and Kochin (1979, p. 474) state: "We have shown that the persistently high rate of unemployment in interwar Britain was due in large part not to deficient aggregate demand but to high unemployment benefits relative to wages."

References

Alchian, Armen 1959: Costs and outputs. In Moses Abramovitz et al. (eds), *The Allocation of Economic Resources*. Stanford: Stanford University Press, 23–40.

Arrow, Kenneth J. 1971: *Essays in the Theory of Risk-bearing*. Chicago: Markham.

Arrow, Kenneth J. 1978: The future and the present in economic life. *Economic Inquiry*, 16, 157–69.

Barro, Robert J. and King, Robert G. Time-separable preferences and inter-temporal-substitution models of business cycles. NBER Working Paper No. 888.

Benjamin, Daniel K. and Kochin, Lewis A. 1979: Searching for an explanation of unemployment in interwar Britain. *Journal of Political Economy*, 87, 441–78.

Burdett, Kenneth and Mortensen, Dale T. 1980: Search, layoffs, and labor market equilibrium. *Journal of Political Economy*, 88, 652–72.

Debreu, Gerard 1959: *Theory of Value: An Axiomatic Analysis of Economic Equilibrium*. New York: Wiley.

Diamond, Peter A. 1967: The role of a stock market in a general equilibrium model with technological uncertainty. *American Economic Review*, 62, 759–78.

Diamond, Peter 1981: Externalities and efficiency in a model of stochastic job matching. Unpublished memorandum.

Fama, Eugene 1970: Multiperiod consumption–investment decisions. *American Economic Review*, 60, 163–74.

Feiger, George 1976: What is speculation? *Quarterly Journal of Economics*, 90, 677–87.

Hayek, Friedrich A. von. 1939: *Profits, Interest, and Investment, and Other Essays on the Theory of Industrial Fluctuations*. London: Routledge & Kegan Paul.

Herberg, Horst 1972: On a two-sector growth model with non-shiftable capital and labour-market imperfections. *Zeitschrift für die Gesamte Staatswissenschaft*, 128, 10–21.

Herberg, Horst and Kemp, Murray C. 1972: Growth and factor market "imperfections." *Zeitschrift für die Gesamte Staatswissenschaft*, 128, 590–604.

Hicks, John R. 1946: *Value and Capital*, 2nd edition. Oxford: Clarendon Press.

Hirshleifer, Jack 1970: *Investment, Interest, and Capital*. Englewood Cliffs, New Jersey: Prentice-Hall.

Hodrick, Robert J. and Prescott, Edward C. 1981: Post-war US business cycles: an empirical investigation. Unpublished memorandum.

Jorgenson, Dale W. 1972: Investment behavior and the production function. *Bell Journal of Economic and Management Science*, 3, 220–51.

Keynes, John Maynard 1936: *The General Theory of Employment, Interest, and Money*. New York: Harcourt, Brace. (First Harbinger edition, 1965.)

King, Robert G. and Plosser, Charles I. 1982: The behavior of money, credit and prices in a real business cycle. NBER Working Paper No. 853.

Krelle, W. 1973: Dynamics of the utility function. In J. R. Hicks and W. Weber (eds), *Carl Menger and the Austrian School of Economics*. London: Oxford University Press, 92–128.

Kydland, Finn 1980: Analysis and policy in competitive models of business fluctuation. Unpublished memorandum.

Kydland, Finn and Prescott, Edward C. 1978: Persistence of unemployment in equilibrium. Unpublished memorandum.

Kydland, Finn E. and Prescott, Edward C. 1980: A competitive theory of fluctuations and the feasibility and desirability of stabilization policy. In Stanley Fischer (ed.), *Rational Expectations and Economic Policy*, Chicago: University of Chicago Press, 169–98.

Kydland, Finn E. and Prescott, Edward C. 1981: Time to build and aggregate fluctuations. Unpublished memorandum.

Leamer, Edward E. 1982: Let's take the con out of econometrics. Unpublished memorandum.

Long, John B. Jr. and Plosser, Charles I. 1982: Real business cycles. Unpublished memorandum.

Lucas, Robert E. Jr. 1967: Adjustment costs and the theory of supply. *Journal of Political Economy*, 75, 321–35.

Lucas, Robert E. Jr. 1975: An equilibrium model of the business cycle. *Journal of Political Economy*, 83, 1113–44.

Lucas, Robert E. Jr. 1977: Understanding business cycles. In Karl Brunner and Allan H. Meltzer (eds), *Stabilization of the Domestic and International Economy*, Volume 5 of the Carnegie-Rochester Conference series on Public Policy. Amsterdam: North-Holland, 7–29.

Lucas, Robert E. Jr. and Prescott, Edward C. 1974: Equilibrium search and unemployment. *Journal of Economic Theory*, 7, 188–209.

Marshak, Jacob 1950: Rational behavior, uncertain prospects, and measurable utility. *Econometrica*, 18, 111–41.

Merton, Robert C. 1973: An intertemporal capital asset pricing model. *Econometrica*, 41, 867–87.

Nelson, Charles R. and Plosser, Charles I. 1981: Trends and random walks in macroeconomic time series: some evidence and implications. Unpublished memorandum.

von Neumann, John and Morgenstern, Oskar 1975: *Theory of Games and Economic Behavior*, 3rd edition. Princeton: Princeton University Press.

Phelps, Edmund S. 1962: The accumulation of risky capital: a sequential utility analysis. *Econometrica*, 30, 729–43. Reprinted in Donald Hester and James Tobin (eds), 1967, *Risk Aversion and Portfolio Choice*. New York: Wiley, 139–53.

Pollack, Robert 1978: Endogenous tastes in demand and welfare analysis. *American Economic Review*, 68, 374–9.

Powell, Alan A. and Gruen, F. H. G. 1968: The constant elasticity of transformation production frontier and linear supply system. *International Economic Review*, 9, 315–28.

Pratt, John W. and Schlaifer, Robert 1982: On the nature and discovery of structure. Unpublished memorandum.

Sargent, Thomas J. 1979: *Macroeconomic Theory*. New York: Academic Press.

Stigler, George J. 1966: *The Theory of Price,* 3rd edition. New York: Macmillan.

Stigler, George J. and Becker, Gary S. 1977: De gustibus non est disputandum. *American Economic Review*, 67, 76–90.

Uzawa, Hirofumi 1969: Time preference and the Penrose effect in a two class model of economic growth. *Journal of Political Economy*, 77, 628–52.

Vickrey, William S. 1964: *Microstatics*. New York: Harcourt, Brace & World.

14

Noise

The effects of noise on the world, and on our views of the world, are profound. Noise in the sense of a large number of small events is often a causal factor much more powerful than a small number of large events can be. Noise makes trading in financial markets possible, and thus allows us to observe prices for financial assets. Noise causes markets to be somewhat inefficient, but often prevents us from taking advantage of inefficiencies. Noise in the form of uncertainty about future tastes and technology by sector causes business cycles, and makes them highly resistant to improvement through government intervention. Noise in the form of expectations that need not follow rational rules causes inflation to be what it is, at least in the absence of a gold standard or fixed exchange rates. Noise in the form of uncertainty about what relative prices would be with other exchange rates makes us think incorrectly that changes in exchange rates or inflation rates cause changes in trade or investment flows or economic activity. Most generally, noise makes it very difficult to test either practical or academic theories about the way that financial or economic markets work. We are forced to act largely in the dark.

Introduction

I use the word "noise" in several senses in this chapter.

In my basic model of financial markets, noise is contrasted with information. People sometimes trade on information in the usual way. They are correct in expecting to make profits from these trades. On the other hand, people sometimes trade on noise as if it were information. If they expect to make profits from noise trading, they are incorrect. However, noise trading is essential to the existence of liquid markets.

Reprinted with permission from *Journal of Finance*, Vol. XLI, No. 3, July, 1986.

In my model of the way we observe the world, noise is what makes our observations imperfect. It keeps us from knowing the expected return on a stock or portfolio. It keeps us from knowing whether monetary policy affects inflation or unemployment. It keeps us from knowing what, if anything, we can do to make things better.

In my model of inflation, noise is the arbitrary element in expectations that leads to an arbitrary rate of inflation consistent with expectations. In my model of business cycles and unemployment, noise is information that hasn't arrived yet. It is simply uncertainty about future demand and supply conditions within and across sectors. When the information does arrive, the number of sectors where there is a good match between tastes and technology is an index of economic activity. In my model of the international economy, changing relative prices become noise that makes it difficult to see that demand and supply conditions are largely independent of price levels and exchange rates. Without these relative price changes, we would see that a version of purchasing power parity holds most of the time.

I think of these models as equilibrium models. Not rational equilibrium models, because of the role of noise and because of the unconventional things I allow an individual's utility to depend on, but equilibrium models nonetheless. They were all derived originally as part of a broad effort to apply the logic behind the capital asset pricing model to markets other than the stock market and to behavior that does not fit conventional notions of optimization.

These models are in very different fields: finance, econometrics, and macroeconomics. Do they have anything in common other than the use of the word "noise" in describing them? The common element, I think, is the emphasis on a diversified array of unrelated causal elements to explain what happens in the world. There is no single factor that causes stock prices to stray from theoretical values, nor even a small number of factors. There is no single variable whose neglect causes econometric studies to go astray. And there is no simple single or multiple factor explanation of domestic or international business fluctuations.

While I have made extensive use of the work of others, I recognize that most researchers in these fields will regard many of my conclusions as wrong, or untestable, or unsupported by existing evidence. I have not been able to think of any conventional empirical tests that would distinguish between my views and the views of others. In the end, my response to the skepticism of others is to make a prediction:

someday, these conclusions will be widely accepted. The influence of noise traders will become apparent. Conventional monetary and fiscal policies will be seen as ineffective. Changes in exchange rates will come to provoke no more comment than changes in the real price of an airline ticket.

Perhaps most important, research will be seen as a process leading to reliable and relevant conclusions only very rarely, because of the noise that creeps in at every step.

If my conclusions are not accepted, I will blame it on noise.

Finance

Noise makes financial markets possible, but also makes them imperfect.[1]

If there is no noise trading, there will be very little trading in individual assets.[2] People will hold individual assets, directly or indirectly, but they will rarely trade them. People trading to change their exposure to broad market risks will trade in mutual funds, or portfolios, or index futures, or index options. They will have little reason to trade in the shares of an individual firm.[3] People who want cash to spend or who want to invest cash they have received will increase or decrease their positions in short-term securities, or money market accounts, or money market mutual funds, or loans backed by real estate or other assets.

A person with information or insights about individual firms will want to trade, but will realize that only another person with information or insights will take the other side of the trade. Taking the other side's information into account, is it still worth trading? From the point of view of someone who knows what both the traders know, one side or the other must be making a mistake.[4] If the one who is making a mistake declines to trade, there will be no trading on information.

In other words, I do not believe it makes sense to create a model with information trading but no noise trading where traders have different beliefs and one trader's beliefs are as good as any other trader's beliefs. Differences in beliefs must derive ultimately from differences in information.[5] A trader with a special piece of information will know that other traders have their own special pieces of information, and will therefore not automatically rush out to trade.

But if there is little or no trading in individual shares, there can be no trading in mutual funds or portfolios or index futures or index options, because there will be no practical way to price them. The whole structure of financial markets depends on relatively liquid markets in the shares of individual firms.

Noise trading provides the essential missing ingredient. Noise trading is trading on noise as if it were information. People who trade on noise are willing to trade even though from an objective point of view they would be better off not trading. Perhaps they think the noise they are trading on is information. Or perhaps they just like to trade.[6]

With a lot of noise traders in the markets, it now pays for those with information to trade. It even pays for people to seek out costly information which they will then trade on. Most of the time, the noise traders as a group will lose money by trading, while the information traders as a group will make money.

The more noise trading there is, the more liquid the markets will be, in the sense of having frequent trades that allow us to observe prices. But noise trading actually puts noise into the prices. The price of a stock reflects both the information that information traders trade on and the noise that noise traders trade on.

As the amount of noise trading increases, it will become more profitable for people to trade on information, but only because the prices have more noise in them. The increase in the amount of information trading does not mean that prices are more efficient. Not only will more information traders come in, but existing information traders will take bigger positions and will spend more on information. Yet prices will be less efficient.[7] What's needed for a liquid market causes prices to be less efficient.

The information traders will not take large enough positions to eliminate the noise. For one thing, their information gives them an edge, but does not guarantee a profit. Taking a larger position means taking more risk. So there is a limit to how large a position a trader will take. For another thing, the information traders can never be sure that they are trading on information rather than noise. What if the information they have has already been reflected in prices? Trading on that kind of information will be just like trading on noise.[8] Because the actual return on a portfolio is a very noisy estimate of expected return, even after adjusting for returns on the market and other factors, it will be difficult to show that information traders have an edge. For the same reason, it will be difficult to show that noise traders are losing by trading. There will always be a lot of ambiguity about who is an information trader and who is a noise trader.

The noise that noise traders put into stock prices will be cumulative, in the same sense that a drunk tends to wander farther and farther from his starting point. Offsetting this, though, will be the research and actions taken by the information traders. The farther the price of a stock gets from its value, the more aggressive the information traders will become. More of them will come in, and they will take larger positions. They may even initiate mergers, leveraged buyouts, and other restructurings.

Thus the price of a stock will tend to move back towards its value over time.[9] The move will often be so gradual that it is imperceptible. If it is fast, technical traders will perceive it and speed it up. If it is slow enough, technical traders will not be able to see it, or will be so unsure of what they see that they will not take large positions.[10]

Still, the farther the price of a stock moves away from value, the faster it will tend to move back. This limits the degree to which it is likely to move away from value. All estimates of value are noisy, so we can never know how far away price is from value.

However, we might define an efficient market as one in which price is within a factor of two of value, i.e., the price is more than half of value and less than twice value.[11] The factor of two is arbitrary, of course. Intuitively, though, it seems reasonable to me, in the light of sources of uncertainty about value and the strength of the forces tending to cause price to return to value. By this definition, I think almost all markets are efficient almost all of the time. "Almost all" means at least 90 percent.

Because value is not observable, it is possible for events that have no information content to affect price. For example, the addition of a stock to the Standard & Poors 500 index will cause some investors to buy it. Their buying will force the price up for a time. Information trading will force it back, but only gradually.[12]

Similarly, when a firm with two classes of common stock issues more of one class, the price of the class of stock issued will decline relative to the price of the class of stock not issued.[13]

Both price and value will look roughly like geometric random walk processes with non-zero means. The means of percentage change in price and value will change over time. The mean of the value process will change because tastes and technology and wealth change. It may well decline when value rises, and rise when value declines. The mean of the price process will change because the relation between price and value changes (and because the mean of the value process changes). Price will tend to move toward value.

The short-term volatility of price will be greater than the short-term volatility of value. Since noise is independent of information in this context, when the variance of the percentage price moves caused by noise is equal to the variance of the percentage price moves caused by information, the variance of percentage price moves from day to day will be roughly twice the variance of percentage value moves from day to day. Over longer intervals, though, the variances will converge. Because price tends to return to value, the variance of price several years from now will be much less than twice the variance of value several years from now.

Volatilities will change over time. The volatility of the value of a firm is affected by things like the rate of arrival of information about the firm and the firm's leverage. All the factors affecting the volatility of a firm's value will change. The volatility of price will change for all these reasons and for other reasons as well. Anything that changes the amount or character of noise trading will change the volatility of price.

Noise traders must trade to have their influence. Because information traders trade with noise traders more than with other information traders, cutting back on noise trading also cuts back on information trading. Thus prices will not move as much when the market is closed as they move when the market is open.[14] The relevant market here is the market on which most of the noise traders trade.

Noise traders may prefer low-priced stocks to high-priced stocks. If they do, then splits will increase both the liquidity of a stock and its day-to-day volatility. Low-priced stocks will be less efficiently priced than high-priced stocks.[15]

The price of a stock will be a noisy estimate of its value. The earnings of a firm (multiplied by a suitable price–earnings ratio) will give another estimate of the value of the firm's stock.[16] This estimate will be noisy too. So long as noise traders do not always look at earnings in deciding how to trade, the estimate from earnings will give information that is not already in the estimate from price.[17]

Because an estimate of value based on earnings will have so much noise, there will be no easy way to use price–earnings ratios in managing portfolios. Even if stocks with low price–earnings ratios have higher expected returns than other stocks, there will be periods, possibly lasting for years, when stocks with low price–earnings ratios have lower returns than other comparable stocks.

In other words, noise creates the opportunity to trade profitably, but at the same time makes it difficult to trade profitably.

Econometrics

Why do people trade on noise?

One reason is that they like to do it. Another is that there is so much noise around that they don't know they are trading on noise. They think they are trading on information.[18]

Neither of these reasons fits into a world where people do things only to maximize expected utility of wealth, and where people always make the best use of available information. Once we let trading enter the utility function directly (as a way of saying that people like to trade), it's hard to know where to stop. If anything can be in the utility function, the notion that people act to maximize expected utility is in danger of losing much of its content.

So we want to be careful about letting things into the utility function. We want to do it only when the evidence is compelling. I believe that this is such a case.

Another such case is dividend payments by firms. Given our tax laws, it seems clear that share repurchase in a non-systematic way is better than payment of dividends. If people want to maximize only expected utility of after-tax wealth, there will be no reason for firms to pay regular dividends. And when they do pay dividends, they will apologize to the stockholders (at least to individual stockholders) for causing them the discomfort of extra taxes.[19]

The idea that dividends convey information beyond that conveyed by the firm's financial statements and public announcements stretches the imagination.[20] It is especially odd that some firms pay dividends while making periodic offerings of common stock that raise more money than the firms are paying in dividends. For such firms, we cannot say that dividends force the firm to go through the rigors of a public offering of stock. Even if they pay no dividends, they will still be issuing common stock.[21]

I think we must assume that investors care about dividends directly. We must put dividends into the utility function.

Perhaps we should be happy that we can continue to think in terms of expected utility at all. There is considerable evidence now that people do not obey the axioms of expected utility. Of special concern is the finding that people will take certain gambles to avoid losses, but will refuse the same gambles when they involve prospective gains. Can this be consistent with risk aversion?[22]

I think that noise is a major reason for the use of decision rules that seem to violate the normal axioms of expected utility. Because there is so much noise in the world, people adopt rules of thumb. They share their rules of thumb with each other, and very few people have enough experience with interpreting noisy evidence to see that the rules are too simple. Over time, I expect that the transmission through the media and through the schools of scientific ways of interpreting evidence will gradually make the rules of thumb more sophisticated, and will thus make the expected utility model more valid.

Even highly trained people, though, seem to make certain kinds of errors consistently. For example, there is a strong tendency in looking at data to assume that when two events frequently happen together, one causes the other. There is an even stronger tendency to assume that the one that occurs first causes the one that occurs second. These tendencies are easy to resist in the simplest cases. But they seem to creep back in when econometric studies become more complex. Sometimes I wonder if we can draw any conclusions at all from the results of regression studies.

Because there is so much noise in the world, certain things are essentially unobservable.

For example, we cannot know what the expected return on the market is. There is every reason to believe that it changes over time, and no particular reason to believe that the changes occur smoothly. We can use the average past return as an estimate of the expected return, but it is a very noisy estimate.[23]

Similarly, the slopes of demand and supply curves are so hard to estimate that they are essentially unobservable. Introspection seems as good a method as any in trying to estimate them. One major problem is that no matter how many variables we include in an econometric analysis, there always seem to be potentially important variables that we have omitted, possibly because they too are unobservable.[24]

For example, wealth is often a key variable in estimating any demand curve. But wealth is itself unobservable. It's not even clear how to define it. The market value of traded assets is part of it, but the value of non-traded assets and especially of human capital is a bigger part for most individuals. There is no way to observe the value of human capital for an individual, and it is not clear how we might go about adding up the values of human capital for individuals to obtain a value of human capital for a whole economy.

I suspect that if it were possible to observe the value of human capital, we would find it fluctuating in much the same way that the level of the stock market fluctuates. In fact, I think we would find fluctuations in the value of human capital to be highly correlated with fluctuations in the level of the stock market, though the magnitude of the fluctuations in the value of human capital is probably less than the magnitude of the fluctuations in the level of the stock market.[25]

It's actually easier to list observables than unobservables, since so many things are unobservable. The interest rate is observable. If there were enough trading in CPI futures, the real interest rate would be observable. So far, though, there are not enough noise traders in CPI futures to make it a viable market.

Stock prices and stock returns are observable. The past volatility of a stock's returns is observable, and by using daily returns we can come close to observing the current volatility of a stock's returns. We can also come close to observing the correlations among the returns on different stocks.

Economic variables seem generally less observable than financial variables. The prices of goods and services are hard to observe, because they are specific to location and terms of trade much more than financial variables. Quantities are hard to observe, because what is traded differs from place to place and through time.

Thus econometric studies involving economic variables are hard to interpret for two reasons: first, the coefficients of regressions tell us little about causal relations even when the variables are observable; and second, the variables are subject to lots of measurement error, and the measurement errors are probably related to the true values of the variables.

Perhaps the easiest economic variable to observe is the money stock, once we agree on a definition for it. I think that accounts for some of the fascination it holds for economic theorists. In my view, though, this easiest to observe of economic variables has no important role in the workings of the economy. Money is still important, but the money stock is not.

Still, the money stock is correlated with every measure of economic activity, because the amount of money used in trade is related to the volume of trade. This correlation implies neither that the government can control the money stock nor that changes in the money stock influence economic activity.[26]

Empirical studies in finance are easier to do than empirical studies in economics, because data on security prices are of generally higher quality than the available data in economics. But there are major pitfalls in trying to interpret even the results of studies of security prices.

For example, many recent empirical studies in finance have taken the form of "event studies," which look at stock price reactions to announcements that affect a firm.[27] If there were no noise in stock prices, this would be a very reliable way to find out how certain events affect firms. In fact, though, the stock price reaction tells us only how investors think the events will affect firms, and investors' thoughts include both noise and information.

Moreover, if investors care directly about certain attributes of a firm (such as its dividend yield) independently of how those attributes affect its value, event studies will pick up these preferences along with the effects of the events on value. When a firm increases its dividend, its price may go up because investors like dividends, even though the present value of its future dividends in a world where the marginal investor is taxed may have gone down.

Is there any solution to these problems? No single, simple solution, I believe. Correlations among economic and financial variables do give us some information of value. Experimental studies in economics and finance have value. Analysis of "stylized facts" is often useful. Unusual events can provide special insight. In the end, a theory is accepted not because it is confirmed by conventional empirical tests, but because researchers persuade one another that the theory is correct and relevant.[28]

Macroeconomics

If business cycles were caused by unanticipated shifts in the general price level or in the level of government spending, we might not call that kind of uncertainty noise. It's too simple. Because it is so simple, I don't think this kind of uncertainty can play a major role in business cycles. I have not seen any models with all the kinds of markets we have in the economy where shifts in the general price level or in the level of government spending are large enough or powerful enough or unanticipated enough to cause significant business cycles.[29]

On the other hand, if business cycles are caused by unanticipated shifts in the entire pattern of tastes and technologies across sectors, we might call that uncertainty noise. I believe that these shifts are significant for the economy as a whole because they do not cancel in any meaningful sense. The number of sectors in which there is a match between tastes and technology varies a lot over time. When it is high, we have an expansion. When it is low, we have a recession.[30]

One reason the shifts do not cancel is that they are not independent across sectors. When the costs of producing goods and services that require oil are high, they will be high across many related sectors. When demand for vacation homes is high, it will be high for many kinds of related services at the same time. The more we divide sectors into subsectors, the more related the subsectors will be to one another.

It is not clear whether the increasing diversity and specialization that go along with the transition from a simple economy to a complex modern economy will be associated with larger or smaller business cycles. On the one hand, the diversity in a more complex economy means that a single crop failure or demand shock cannot have such a devastating effect; but on the other hand, the specialization in a more complex economy means that when there is a mismatch between tastes and technology, it is costly to move skills and machines between sectors to correct the mismatch.

Money and prices play no role in this explanation. Everything is real.[31] For a small sample of the kind of thing I have in mind, suppose I gear up to produce dolls, while you gear up to produce art books. If it turns out that you want dolls and I want art books, we will have a boom. We will both work hard, and will exchange our outputs, and will have high consumption of both dolls and art books. But if it turns out that you want action toys and I want science books, we will have a bust. The relative price of toys and books may be the same as before, but neither of us will work so hard because we will not value highly that which we can exchange our outputs for.

This is just one kind of example. The variations can occur in use of machines as well as in use of people, and the underlying uncertainty can concern what we can make as well as what we want.

Unanticipated shifts in tastes and technology within and across sectors is what we call information in discussing financial markets. In economic markets, it seems more appropriate to call these shifts noise, to contrast them with shifts in the aggregates that conventional macroeconomic models focus on. In other words, the cause of business cycles is not a few large things that can be measured and controlled, but many small things that are difficult to measure and essentially impossible to control.

Noise or uncertainty has its effects in economic markets because there are costs in shifting physical and human resources within and between sectors. If skills and capital can be shifted without cost after tastes and technology become known, mismatches between what we can do and what we want to do will not occur.

The costs of shifting real resources are clearly large, so it is plausible that these costs might play a role in business cycles. The costs of putting inflation adjustments in contracts or of publicizing changes in the money stock or the price level seem low, so it is not plausible that these costs play a significant role in business cycles.

Presumably the government does not have better information about the details of future supply and demand conditions within and between sectors than the people working in those sectors. Thus there is little the government can do to help the economy avoid recessions. These unknown future details are noise to the workers and managers involved, and they are noise twice over to government employees, even those who collect statistics on individual industries.

I cannot think of any conventional econometric tests that would shed light on the question of whether my business cycle theory is correct or not. One of its predictions, though, is that real wages will fluctuate with other measures of economic activity. When there is a match between tastes and technology in many sectors, income will be high, wages will be high, output will be high, and unemployment will be low. Thus real wages will by procyclical. This is obviously true over long periods, as from the 1920s to the 1930s and from the 1930s to the 1940s, but it also seems true over shorter periods, especially when overtime and layoffs are taken into account.[32]

How do inflation and money fit into this picture?

I believe that monetary policy is almost completely passive in a country like the US.[33] Money goes up when prices go up or when income goes up because demand for money goes up at those times. I have been unable to construct an equilibrium model in which changes in money cause changes in prices or income, but I have had no trouble constructing an equilibrium model in which changes in prices or income cause changes in money.[34]

Changes in money often precede changes in income, but this is not surprising, since demand for money can depend on expected income as well as current income. Changes in wealth (measured at market value) also precede changes in income.

In the conventional story, open market operations change perceived wealth, which leads to a change in demand for existing assets, and thus to a change in the price level. But open market operations have no effect on wealth when wealth is measured at market value. They merely substitute one form of wealth for another. Some say that open market operations cause a change in interest rates, which then have further effects on the economy. But this cannot happen in an equilibrium model. There is no temporary equilibrium, with the price level and rate of inflation unchanged, where a different interest rate will be equal to the certain component of the marginal product of capital. If we allow the price level and rate of inflation to change, then there are many equilibria, but there are no rules to tell us how one is chosen over another. There is no logical story explaining how the change in money will cause a shift from one equilibrium to another.

If monetary policy doesn't cause changes in inflation, what does?

I think that the price level and rate of inflation are literally indeterminate. They are whatever people think they will be. They are determined by expectations, but expectations follow no rational rules. If people believe that certain changes in the money stock will cause changes in the rate of inflation, that may well happen, because their expectations will be built into their long-term contracts.

Another way to make the same point is this. Within a sector, the prices of inputs and outputs are largely taken as given. Decisions on what and how much to produce are made taking these prices as given. Thus each sector assumes that the rates of inflation of its input and output prices are given. In my models, this includes the government sector in its role as supplier of money. If we are in an equilibrium with one expected rate of inflation (assuming neither gold prices nor exchange rates are fixed), and everyone shifts to a lower expected rate of inflation, we will have (with only minor modifications) a new equilibrium.

One way to describe this view is to say that noise causes changes in the rate of inflation.

If we have a gold standard, where the price of gold is adjusted over time to make the general price level follow a desired path, and where the government stands ready to buy or sell gold at the temporarily fixed price without allowing its inventory to fluctuate much, then inflation will be controlled rather than random.[35] But it seems unlikely that we will adopt a gold standard of this kind or of any other kind anytime soon.

Similarly, if a small country adopts a policy of varying its exchange rate with a large country to make its price level follow a desired path, where its government stands ready to buy or sell foreign exchange at the temporarily fixed rate without allowing its foreign exchange inventory to fluctuate much, then its inflation rate will be controlled rather than random. This is possible for any country that has wealth and stable taxing power, because the country can always sell assets for foreign exchange, and can then buy the assets back (almost) with the foreign currency it obtains.

However, it is not clear what is gained by controlling the price level. If business cycles are caused by real factors rather than by things that are affected by the rate of inflation, then many of the reasons for controlling inflation vanish.

In my view, then, there is a real international equilibrium that is largely unaffected by price levels or monetary policies, except in countries with unstable financial markets or national debt that is large compared with taxable wealth. This real equilibrium involves a world business cycle and national business cycles driven by the degree to which there is a match between tastes and technology.

The real equilibrium also involves changing relative prices for all kinds of goods and services, including relative prices for the "same" goods and services in different locations. Different locations can be around the corner or around the world. Since information and transportation are so costly (especially information), there is no form of arbitrage that will force the prices of similar goods and services in different locations to be similar.

Moreover, the real equilibrium involves constantly changing trade flows for various pairs of countries. There is no reason for trade to be balanced between any pair of countries either in the short run or in the long run. And an imbalance in trade has no particular welfare implications.[36]

Since the real equilibrium is fixed at a point in time, though it is continually changing through time, a higher domestic currency price for an item at one point in time will mean a higher domestic currency price for all items at that same point in time. There will be some lags in making price changes, and many lags in posting or reporting price changes, but these will not affect the equilibrium significantly.

If we were able to observe the economy at a given point in time with two different domestic price levels, we would see that the real equilibrium is largely independent of price levels and exchange rates, and we might call this situation "purchasing power parity." Since we must actually observe the economy as it evolves over time, we cannot see that purchasing power parity holds. We see relative price changes occurring, and fluctuations in the level of economic activity, while exchange rates and money stocks are changing. We think that exchange rates and money are causing relative price changes and business fluctuations.[37]

But that is only because the noise in the data is clouding our vision.

I am grateful for comments on earlier drafts by Peter Bernstein, Robert Merton, James Poterba, Richard Roll, Hersh Shefrin, Meir Statman, Lawrence Summers, and Laurence Weiss.

Notes

1 The concept of noise trading and its role in financial markets that I develop in this chapter was developed through conversations with James Stone.

2 Jaffe and Winkler (1976) have a model where the traders who make speculative markets stable are those who trade to adjust their risk levels or who misperceive their forecasting abilities or who trade for reasons other than maximizing expected return for a given level of risk. Figlewski (1978) has a model where there are two types of traders who differ in forecasting ability. Since neither kind of trader explicitly takes into account the information the other kind of trader has, each is to some degree trading on noise.

3 Rubinstein (1975), Milgrom and Stokey (1982), and Hakansson, Kunkel, and Ohlson (1982) show in a state preference world that differences in information may affect prices without causing people to trade. Grossman and Stiglitz (1980) show that there may be no equilibrium when rational investors trade in the market portfolio. Grossman (1978) shows the same thing for a world with trading in individual assets. Diamond and Verrecchia (1981) redefine a rational expectations equilibrium in the presence of noise and show the conditions under which their equilibrium exists. In Tirole's model (1982), "speculation" relies on inconsistent plans, and thus is ruled out by rational expectations. Kyle (1984, 1985a, 1985b) and Grinblatt and Ross (1985) look at quite different models of equilibrium where traders have market power. Kyle specifically examines the effects of changing the number of noise traders in both kinds of equilibrium.

4 This assumes that the traders start with well-diversified portfolios. In Admati (1985), the traders start with suboptimal portfolios of assets.

5 Varian (1985) distinguishes between "opinions" and "information." He says that only differences in opinions will generate trading. In the kind

of model he is working with, I think that differences of opinion will not exist.

6 In Laffont (1985), traders gather costly information because it has direct utility for reasons other than trading. Once they have it, they trade on it. If people start with efficient portfolios, though, even the arrival of free information may not make them want to trade. We may need to introduce direct utility of trading to explain the existence of speculative markets.

7 This result is specific to a model where noise traders trade on noise as if it were information. In Kyle's (1984, 1985a, 1985b) model, having more noise traders can make markets more efficient.

8 Arrow (1982) says that excessive reaction to current information characterizes all the securities and future markets. If this is true, it could be caused by trading on information that has already been discounted.

9 Merton (1971) describes a model where long-run prices are efficient but short-run prices need not be.

10 Summers (1986) emphasizes the difficulty in telling whether markets are efficient or not. This difficulty affects market participants and researchers alike.

11 I think this puts me between Merton (1985) and Shiller (1981, 1984). Deviations from efficiency seem more significant in my world than in Merton's, but much less significant in my world than in Shiller's.

12 This effect was discovered independently by Shleifer (1986) and Gurel and Harris (1985).

13 Loderer and Zimmermann (1985) discovered this effect in connection with offerings in Switzerland, where multiple classes of stock are common.

14 French and Roll (1985) find that the volatilities of stock returns are much lower across periods when markets are closed than across periods when markets are open.

15 Ohlson and Penman (1985) find that when stocks split, their return volatilities go up on the ex-split date by an average of about 30 percent. This may be due to a higher proportion of noise traders, though they also find no increase in trading volume on the ex-split date. Amihud (1985) feels that another possible explanation for this result is the increase in the bid-asked spread following a stock split.

16 For a discussion of the relation between earnings and stock price, see Black (1980).

17 Basu (1983) summarizes the evidence that stocks with high earnings–price ratios have higher expected returns than stocks with low earnings–price ratios, even after controlling for size of firm and risk. DeBondt and Thaler (1985) give more evidence on the existence of temporary dislocations in price and on the psychological factors that may influence the noise traders who create these opportunities.

18 Kahneman and Tversky (1979) have a more sophisticated model of why people make decisions for what are seemingly non-rational reasons. Their

theory may help describe the motivation of noise traders. For applications of their theory to economics and finance, see Russell and Thaler (1985).

19 In Black (1978a), I described the dividend puzzle. The solution to the puzzle, I now believe, is that we must put dividends directly into the utility function. For one way of putting dividends into the utility function, see Shefrin and Statman (1985). For another way of resolving the dividend puzzle, and of relating it to the capital structure puzzle, see Myers (1984).

20 For a statement of the case that dividends do convey information, see Miller (1985).

21 Kalay and Shimrat (1985) observe, however, that firms issuing common stock do tend to reduce their dividends.

22 This phenomenon is discussed extensively by Tversky and Kahneman (1981).

23 Merton (1980) shows how difficult it is to estimate the expected return on the market.

24 Chapter 12 and Leamer (1983) discuss the profound difficulties with conventional econometric analyses.

25 Fama and Schwert (1977) study the relation between human capital and the stock market. They do not find a close relation.

26 King and Plosser (1984) look at the possibility that economic activity influences the money stock rather than the other way round.

27 For a typical event study, together with discussion of a factor that may make event studies hard to interpret properly, see Kalay and Loewenstein (1985).

28 This point of view is taken in part from McCloskey (1983).

29 For a review of research in business cycle theory, see Zarnowitz (1985). For an attempt to explain large business cycles with seemingly innocent changes in the price level see Mankiw (1985).

30 For a more extensive discussion of this point of view, see chapters 10 and 12.

31 The most closely related work in the more conventional business cycle literature is Long and Plosser (1983) and Lilien (1982). Bernanke (1983) has an entirely real explanation for swings in the production of durable goods: it is sectoral in the sense that specific investments are irreversible. Topel and Weiss (1985) use uncertainty about employment conditions in different sectors to help explain unemployment; their methods can also be applied, I think, to explaining cyclical fluctuations in unemployment.

32 Bils (1985) reviews previous work in this area, and gives evidence that real wages are indeed procyclical.

33 My views are explained more fully in chapters 1, 2, and 4.

34 For an analysis of possible explanations for some of the correlations between money and other variables, see Cornell (1983).

35 For an old version of this argument, see Fisher (1920). For a new version, together with discussion of the possibility of keeping gold inventories roughly fixed while controlling the price of gold and the price level, see chapter 11.

36 This is a common result in international economics. For my treatment of it, see Black (1978b).
37 Davutyan and Pippenger (1985) suggest some ways in which standard tests of purchasing power parity may be flawed. Moreover, our tests of purchasing power parity are inadequate unless we consider transport costs, as Aizenman (1984) notes. Transport costs can be very large for services and some goods.

References

Admati, Anat R. 1985: A noisy rational expectations equilibrium for multi-asset securities markets. *Econometrica* 53, 629–57.

Aizenman, Joshua 1984: Testing deviations from purchasing power parity (PPP). National Bureau of Economic Research Working Paper No. 1475.

Amihud, Yakov 1985: Biases in computed return variance: an application to volatility increases subsequent to stock splits. Unpublished manuscript.

Arrow, Kenneth J. 1982: Risk perception in psychology and economics. *Economic Inquiry*, 20, 1–9.

Basu, Sanjoy 1983: The relationship between earnings' yield, market value and return for NYSE common stocks: further evidence. *Journal of Financial Economics*, 12, 129–56.

Bernanke, Ben S. 1983: Irreversibility, uncertainty, and cyclical investment. *Quarterly Journal of Economics* (Feb. 1983) 85–106.

Bils, Mark J. 1985: Real wages over the business cycle: evidence from panel data. *Journal of Political Economy*, 93, 666–89.

Black, Fischer 1978a: The dividend puzzle. *Journal of Portfolio Management*, 2, 5–8.

Black, Fischer 1978b: The ins and outs of foreign investment. *Financial Analysts Journal*, 34, 25–32.

Black, Fischer 1980: The magic in earnings: economic earnings versus accounting earnings. *Financial Analysts Journal*, 36, 19–24.

Cornell, Bradford 1983: The money supply announcements puzzle: review and interpretation. *American Economic Review*, 73, 644–57.

Davutyan, Nurhan and Pippenger, John 1985: Purchasing power parity did not collapse during the 1970's. *American Economic Review*, 75, 1151--8.

DeBondt, Werner F. M. and Thaler, Richard 1985: Does the stock market overreact? *Journal of Finance*, 40, 793–805.

Diamond, Douglas W. and Verrecchia, Robert E. 1981: Information aggregation in noisy rational expectations economy. *Journal of Financial Economics*, 9, 221–35.

Fama, Eugene F. and Schwert, G. William 1977: Human capital and capital market equilibrium. *Journal of Financial Economics*, 4, 95–125.

Figlewski, Stephen 1978: Market "efficiency" in a market with heterogeneous information. *Journal of Political Economy*, 86, 581–97.

Fisher, Irving 1920: *Stabilizing the Dollar*. New York: Macmillan.

French, Kenneth R. and Roll, Richard 1985: Stock return variances: the arrival of information and the reaction of traders. Graduate School of Management, UCLA Working Paper.

Grinblatt, Mark S. and Ross, Stephen A. 1985: Market power in a securities market with endogenous information. *Quarterly Journal of Economics*, 100, 1143–67.

Grossman, Sanford 1978: Further results on the informational efficiency of competitive stock markets. *Journal of Economic Theory*, 18, 81–101.

Grossman, Sanford and Stiglitz, Joseph E. On the impossibility of informationally efficient markets. *American Economic Review*, 70, 393–408.

Gurel, Eitan and Harris, Lawrence 1985: Price and volume effects associated with changes in the S&P 500 list: new evidence for the existence of price pressures. Unpublished manuscript.

Hakansson, Nils, Kunkel, J. Gregory and Ohlson, James 1982: Sufficient and necessary conditions for information to have social value in pure exchange. *Journal of Finance*, 37, 1169–81.

Jaffe, Jeffrey F. and Winkler, Robert L. 1976: Optimal speculation against an efficient market. *Journal of Finance*, 31, 49–61.

Kahneman, Daniel and Tversky, Amos 1979: Prospect theory: an analysis of decision under risk. *Econometrica*, 47, 263–91.

Kalay, Avner and Shimrat, Adam 1985: On the payment of equity financed dividends. Unpublished manuscript.

Kalay, Avner and Loewenstein, Uri 1985: Predictable events and excess returns: the case of dividend announcements. *Journal of Financial Economics*, 14, 423–49.

King, Robert G. and Plosser, Charles I. 1984: Money, credit, and prices in a real business cycle. *American Economic Review*, 74, 360–80.

Kyle, Albert S. 1984: Market structure, information, futures markets, and price formation. In Gary G. Storey, Andrew Schmitz, and Alexander H. Sarris (eds), *International Agricultural Trade*. Boulder and London: Westview Press, 45–63.

Kyle, Albert S. 1985a: Continuous auctions and insider trading. *Econometrica*, 53, 1315–35.

Kyle, Albert S. 1985b: Informed speculation with imperfect competition. Unpublished manuscript.

Laffont, Jean-Jacques 1985: On the welfare analysis of rational expectations equilibria with asymmetric information. *Econometrica*, 53, 1–29.

Leamer, Edward E. 1983: Let's take the con out of econometrics. *American Economic Review*, 73, 31–43.

Lilien, David M. 1982: Sectoral shifts and cyclical unemployment. *Journal of Political Economy*, 90, 777–93.

Lilien, David M. 1982: A sectoral model of the business cycle. USC Modelling Research Group Working Paper no. 8231.

Loderer, Claudio and Zimmermann, Heinz 1985: Rights issues in Switzerland: some findings to consider in the debate over financing decisions. Unpublished manuscript.

Long, John B. Jr. and Plosser, Charles I. 1983: Real business cycles. *Journal of Political Economy*, 91, 39–69.

Mankiw, N. Gregory 1985: Small menu costs and large business cycles. *Quarterly Journal of Economics*, 100, 529–38.

McCloskey, Donald N. 1983: The rhetoric of economics. *Journal of Economic Literature*, 21, 481–517.

Merton, Robert C. 1971: Optimum consumption and portfolio rules in a continuous-time model. *Journal of Economic Theory*, 3, 373–413.

Merton, Robert C. 1980: On estimating the expected return on the market: an exploratory investigation. *Journal of Financial Economics*, 8, 323–61.

Merton, Robert C. 1985: On the current state of the stock market rationality hypothesis. Sloan School of Management Working Paper no. 1717–85.

Milgrom, Paul and Stokey, Nancy 1982: Information, trade and common knowledge. *Journal of Economic Theory*, 26, 17–27.

Miller, Merton H. 1985: The information content of dividends. Unpublished manuscript.

Myers, Stewart C. 1984: The capital structure puzzle. *Journal of Finance*, 39, 575–92.

Ohlson, James A. and Penman, Stephen H. 1985: Volatility increases subsequent to stock splits: an empirical aberration. *Journal of Financial Economics*, 14, 251–66.

Rubinstein, Mark 1975: Security market efficiency in an Arrow-Debreu economy. *American Economic Review*, 65, 812–24.

Russell, Thomas and Thaler, Richard 1985: The relevance of quasi rationality in competitive markets. *American Economic Review*, 75, 1071–82.

Shefrin, Hersh and Statman, Meir 1985: Comparing two theories of dividend function. Unpublished manuscript.

Shiller, Robert J. 1981: Do stock prices move too much to be justified by subsequent changes in dividends? *American Economic Review*, 71, 421–36.

Shiller, Robert J. 1984: Stock prices and social dynamics. *Brookings Papers on Economic Activity*, 2, 457–98.

Shleifer, Andrei 1986: Do demand curves for stocks slope down? *Journal of Finance*, 41, 579–90.

Summers, Lawrence H. 1986: Do we really know that financial markets are efficient? *Journal of Finance*, 41, 591–602.

Tirole, Jean 1982: On the possibility of speculation under rational expectations. *Econometrica*, 50, 1163–81.

Topel, Robert and Weiss, Laurence 1985: Sectoral uncertainty and unemployment. University of California at San Diego Economics Department Discussion Paper 85–27.

Tversky, Amos and Kahneman, Daniel 1981: The framing of decisions and the psychology of choice. *Science*, 211, 453-8.

Varian, Hal R. 1985: Differences of opinion and the volume of trade. University of Michigan Department of Economics Discussion Paper C-67.

Zarnowitz, Victor 1985: Recent work on business cycles in historical perspective: a review of theories and evidence. *Journal of Economic Literature*, 23, 523-80.

Index